Community Theatres

Theatre and Stage Series

Community Theatres

Percy Corry

with designs by Robert Adams

 Pitman Publishing

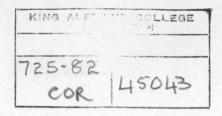
First published, 1974

Sir Isaac Pitman and Sons Ltd
Pitman House, Parker Street, Kingsway, London WC2B 5PB
Banda Street, PO Box 46038, Nairobi, Kenya

Sir Isaac Pitman (Aust) Pty Ltd
Pitman House, 158 Bouverie Street, Carlton, Victoria 3053, Australia

Pitman Publishing Corporation
6 East 43rd Street, New York, NY 10017, USA

Sir Isaac Pitman (Canada) Ltd
495 Wellington Street West, Toronto 135, Canada

The Copp Clark Publishing Company
517 Wellington Street West, Toronto 135, Canada

Typeset by Print Origination, Bootle, Lancs, L20 6NS
Printed in Great Britain
By Unwin Brothers Limited
The Gresham Press, Old Woking, Surrey, England
A member of the Staples Printing Group.
G3509: 13

Preface

It was originally intended that this book should be concerned primarily with the planning of theatre buildings and the stage equipment to be put in them, to replace *Planning the Stage*, a book which I wrote in 1959, now very much out of date and mercifully out of print. A particular type of theatre was chosen and, as argument and facts were marshalled, it was realized that the book should be aimed not only at the people concerned in the design and planning of the building but also at those engaged in planning *for* such a building, the people who wished to have a theatre for use by their local community. The projects with which I had been associated had emphasized the need for some such attempt at guidance.

Much of the comment is inevitably statement of personal opinion based on quite extensive experience but I realize that, although an attempt has been made to be impartial and objective, it is quite likely that there will be conflicting opinions from others with like experience. One cannot obscure one's personal convictions and prejudices and it would probably be rather dull if one did.

I would offer gratitude to the many people on whose assistance I have relied and in particular to Robert Adams, who has been responsible for most of the drawings, including the plans for the theoretical project. He has collaborated with unfailing courtesy and good humour despite the many alterations and additions caused by the author's infuriating changes of mind—infuriating, that is, to the author himself; they involved a great deal of rewriting. My thanks are also due to my friend and former colleague, Frederick Bentham, and to Rank Strand Electric for permission to quote from *TABS* and to reproduce illustrations; to the Arts Council for permission to quote from *The Theatre Today in England and Wales;* to the Director-General of the Greater London Council for permission to reproduce the photograph of the Lyric Theatre, Hammersmith; to Elizabeth Sweeting for permission to quote from *Theatre Administration;* to Hall Stage Equipment Ltd for drawings and photographs of various items of stage equipment; to Les Jobson for information about the activities in Billingham Forum; and not least, to my editor, Ian Herbert, for his patient toleration of my repeated delays in supplying the script.

Percy Corry

Contents

Illustrations

1
Introductory

The term "Community Theatre" is not yet self-explanatory in Britain. The name is used here to describe a theatre-type of building provided by the community for use by all sections of the community both as audiences and as performers. The Community Theatre must serve not only as a playhouse but for a number of very varied activities and, because there is an obvious need, many such theatres will be built.

The purpose of this book is to discuss the problems of those who have to decide what types of theatres should be authorized and financed, and also to consider the practical implications for those who are asked to plan and equip the buildings. The former are susceptible to pressures from interested parties with conflicting opinions and are liable to be influenced by the arguments most plausibly presented or, more probably, by the lowest estimate of cost, which may well be based on the least suitable project.

Before considering the need for and the requirements of the Community Theatre it may be useful to glance at the current pattern of theatre in Britain, a pattern not very different from that in other English-speaking countries.

The Commercial Theatre

Before the professional theatre was subjected to the serious competition of the cinema, and later of television, it was run almost completely as a highly speculative business financed by private individuals or companies. Its purpose was to sell live entertainment as profitably as possible.

In most areas it is now impossible to sell such theatre performances to audiences large enough in total to earn even a modest profit after paying the rapidly increasing costs. Consequently, most of the theatres that operated profitably, albeit rather precariously, during the early years of the century, have now ceased to exist. In the West End of London, in a few provincial cities and in popular seaside holiday towns the large commercial theatres still manage to keep open but most of the population of the country have no professional theatre within reasonable distance of their homes. Formerly, the provincial towns were served by professional touring companies, many of them operating from metropolitan bases, often including star actors and making regular visits to what were known as No.1 theatres in the large towns. Touring is now very expensive and, as it has always been arduous, actors are not eager to leave the capital or the other film and television centres where there could be greater prospect of engagement.

As the number of theatres has progressively diminished the touring companies have almost disappeared and the few remaining provincial theatres find it impossible to book sufficient compelling attractions to enable them to keep open all the year round. The position now appears to be changing since the jobs for actors in films and television are becoming fewer and there are signs of a greater willingness to tour the provinces if new theatres are able to offer the prospect of good contracts.

In 1970 the Arts Council of Great Britain issued its report of an inquiry into the state of the professional theatre in England and Wales under the title "The Theatre Today." One of the recommendations of the Committee of inquiry proposed the establishment of a Theatre Investment Fund, partially subsidized by the Arts Council, to finance tours to a circuit of the remaining No.1 theatres. This Committee, with rather pessimistic realism, assumed that only about twelve such theatres could survive and even those, it was suggested, would have to be owned and partly subsidized by Local Authorities. It is not possible to say how far such an Investment Fund could become effective but recognition of the principle of stimulating the return of touring companies could be important. The Committee did not suggest any development of touring companies for the smaller theatres but, whatever the fate of the Investment Fund idea, it will be necessary, sooner or later, to consider development of a possible market that could be larger than the No.1 circuit.

The old Variety Theatres—formerly known as Music Halls—have almost disappeared but individual acts of the type that would have toured those theatres are now booked by clubs and restaurants in which customers eat and/or drink during performances. Music Hall has thus turned full circle and is back to a modern equivalent of the pubs in which it formerly flourished. It is a form of theatre which survives as a commercial proposition. In its more lush forms it has a profitable expense-account clientele.

The Subsidized Theatre

It is now realized that most professional theatres, like concert halls, libraries, art galleries, museums and a number of other recreational and cultural institutions, depend for continued existence on some form of communal subsidy. This has long been recognized in the cases of opera, ballet and the leading orchestras, as the costs involved are far in excess of potential revenue from the sale of seats. The social necessity for maintaining and extending minority cultural activities is being officially accepted, if with something less than reckless enthusiasm.

The sources of subsidies vary. The money may be provided by the State, by Local

Authorities, by foundations created by wealthy patrons or by a combination of such sources. In Britain the main subsidizing authority is the Arts Council, which distributes funds provided by the national exchequer. It is often argued that too great a proportion of the limited funds available is given to the prestigious metropolitan companies (about half of the national funds allocated), and that contributions to the provinces are comparatively meagre. Local Authorities are, however, expected to supplement the national subsidies; they do so without any uniformity of generosity or parsimony. The national subsidies available for provincial theatres are paid mainly to those with resident repertory companies, which appear, on average, to meet between 50 and 75 per cent of their running costs by box-office and bar receipts. During the ten years from 1959 onwards the number of such repertory theatres increased from 28 to 52, an increase claimed to be largely due to assistance from public funds.

The Arts Council report already referred to states: "The future of the theatre outside London will be mainly determined by the Local Authorities. Their partnership with the Arts Council is certainly stronger than it used to be but their level of patronage still falls far short of what was envisaged in the Local Government Act of 1948. They have lately undertaken in some towns the responsibility of taking over the No.1 touring theatres from their former commercial owners and to that extent are accepting a new commitment. This, coupled with their support for the Reps, makes them the decisive arbiter of the theatre's destiny outside London and this responsibility is going to cost them considerably more than the best of them spends at present."

The Amateur Theatre

Although precise figures are not available, it has been estimated that in Britain something like 30,000 amateur companies of varying size and quality play with some regularity to audiences that probably exceed in total the audiences of the professional theatres. The amateur companies are not usually subsidized; they rely on box-office receipts being supplemented by their members' annual subscriptions, and by contributions to all kinds of ingenious social functions devised to keep the profit and loss account out of the red.

For a majority of the population amateur companies provide the only live theatrical performances they are able to attend within reasonable distance of their homes. The companies vary from small groups playing in village halls and schools to large companies presenting musical shows to audiences of thousands.

There are also amateurs who own their purpose-built theatres in which they stage very efficiently seven or eight, or even more, productions each year. Too many companies, however, are compelled to play in unsuitable and badly equipped multi-purpose halls. Some of the larger musical societies are now finding it difficult or impossible to rent suitable accommodation owing to the closing of theatres and cinemas in which they previously put on their shows.

It is reasonable to expect that the inevitable increase in leisure time will stimulate amateur activity if the accommodation is available. Schools and colleges devote a lot of time and energy to the performing arts but much of the interest created is wasted if there is too little provision for later adult participation, whether as audiences or performers.

A Community Theatre is not necessarily a substitute for a theatre that has a resident professional repertory company. Even the large urban areas which already have resident professional companies also need Community Theatres. In the smaller areas, unable to support resident companies, the Community Theatre should cater for regular visits by touring professional performers. Creation of a circuit of Community Theatres could foster close liaison between professionals and amateurs, with benefit to both.

The following further quotation from the Arts Council report is interesting:

"The rapid increase of Reps in the last ten years or so has led some observers, including experienced and sympathetic ones, to wonder whether the parable of the mustard-tree is not more apt than the fairy tale about the bean-stalk. Has Britain the capacity to sustain fifty Reps in terms of talent, 'product', audience or finance? This question provokes conflicting answers. The perfectionists assert that there is not, and cannot be, enough 'good theatre' to maintain so many Reps and the more fervent of them quote Gresham's Law on this issue. They maintain that the health of the theatre would be better assured by a limited number of major theatres, strongholds of quality equipped to achieve superlative standards, regional festival theatres rather than workaday Reps."

The Community Theatre could probably help to bridge the gap between two conflicting points of view, neither of which appears to be much concerned with the amateurs. Professional and amateur theatre should be complementary; both are essential. The professional theatre could possibly recognize this in two ways, with benefit to itself and to the community in general.

1. New or existing companies could organize productions to tour the Community Theatres on a national or regional basis and on a scale suited to economic travel. A number of companies do operate limited and partially subsidized tours but are often compelled to travel uneconomic distances and to play under frustrating conditions.

2. It is suggested that in each region there should ultimately be a permanent repertory theatre, designed and equipped to have two or more productions in operation concurrently. The staff employed would be sufficient to provide continuity of performances in the home theatre while one or more companies toured. The personnel would be interchangeable between the companies and any production intended for tour would first be staged in the home theatre. As the number of Community Theatres increased, the distances to be travelled could decrease and in time each regional Repertory Theatre could have its own circuit of new theatres whose audiences would look forward to welcoming their favourite performers on regular

visits. In some regions the Community Theatres could be within such a radius that the companies could have permanent living accommodation in the base towns, travelling daily by motor coach to and from the theatres visited.

There have been experiments in this direction. Also, a number of established theatres have teams of actors who visit schools to give performances which, it is argued, help to create the audiences of tomorrow. Obviously, it would be of greater value if a greater number of children were able to enjoy well-staged performances in modern theatres. The few professional companies which specialize in theatre for young people have done valuable work with small companies of under-paid actors working with limited facilities. The Community Theatre is the obvious place for Children's Theatre which, given the opportunity that circuits of such theatres would provide, could enlarge the scale and the scope of their work.

In recent years there has been some argument in favour of allowing schools to be used more extensively by adults for cultural activities during periods when the schools would otherwise be closed. Such additional use may be helpful in spreading capital and running costs but the facilities likely to be available for adult activities are usually too restricted. In the larger urban areas the schools are necessarily scattered and appeal is likely to be very localized. Such a school scheme could be supplementary to, but not a substitute for, a Community Theatre which should be centrally situated and should attract the residents of the whole area. It could be a better relationship of cart and horse if the students of the schools were to be encouraged to use the special facilities of the Community Theatre in addition to the more instructional use of their own drama studios and stages.

Ideally, the Community Theatre should be part of a comprehensive centre in which old and young could share in all kinds of leisure pursuits in congenial surroundings. There should be accommodation for all the visual and performing arts; the theatre should be a dominant feature and its relationship to any possible future additions would need careful planning. In the selection of a site it is worth considering the example set by the City of Birmingham in allocating fourteen acres of their Cannon Hill Park for the building of an extensive Arts Centre for young people. Most urban areas have parks which are used only in daylight hours. It could be sensible and probably more economical to extend the social usefulness of such valuable and attractive sites outside expensive development areas, provided they are easily accessible.

A Community Theatre is being gradually accepted more as a necessity than as a luxury. The organizations and individuals likely to be most concerned should do something about it. It is useless to wait passively for a benevolent authority to anticipate (and possibly misunderstand) their needs. They should state them in specific and practical terms. The co-operation of any national organizations to which they may be affiliated could be useful.

If the Community Theatre is to develop maximum value it must have the widest possible appeal. It must not be exclusive or "arty and crafty." It should accept with impartial goodwill the red-nosed comic (or his current equivalent) and the classical tragedian, the strident pop group and the genteel string quartet. The theatre will best serve its community if it is seen to be a vital and versatile section of a lively organization that is efficiently catering for the greatest possible variety of leisure activities of the surrounding citizenry.

An interesting and comprehensive community centre was built in 1967 in the small town of Billingham in County Durham. The following report on its opening was published in *TABS* (the Strand Electric journal) in December 1967 (Vol. 25, No. 4):

"This Forum represents a novel and stimulating use by the council of a small town of parliament's paternal permission to use its own ratepayers' money for their recreation and entertainment. Billingham is an expanding township of some 35,000 people, ringed about by Tees-side's dark satanic industrial plants, a widespread demolition and 'development' of part of our Jerusalem of anonymous mediocrity. It is but a few miles from Stockton-on-Tees, Middlesbrough, the Hartlepools and other less known urban areas that have obliterated much of North-east England's green and pleasant Cleveland.

"Billingham is well justified in claiming that their Forum is truly a community centre. It is described as 'a meeting place or centre for the community's leisure, recreation and artistic appreciation.' Although it justified an official opening by the Queen it has received scant publicity nationally, due no doubt to the usual metropolitan myopia in viewing the provinces in the remote north. This is, in fact, a courageous example that could well be followed by other towns where there is the sort of enthusiasm and vision that have brought the Billingham Forum into being.

"It is amazingly comprehensive: in current jargon it could be described as a complex of four main buildings. It caters for 25 listed games and sports as well as for 'Theatre, Cinema and the Arts.' Extensive but of no very obvious complexity. There is a Sports Hall 120 ft by 60 ft for gymnastics, tennis badminton, netball, etc. Another hall 115 ft by 14 ft caters for Indoor bowls (not mechanized skittles); archery, cricket, golf and shooting can be practised in a hall 100 ft by 24 ft. A small 40 ft square room will accommodate all kinds of activities by the interchange of the necessary props such as judo mats, tennis tables, weights for lifting, foils for fencing and so on; there are three squash courts. An international size ice-rink has a seating capacity of 1,000; the ice can be removed to provide an arena for competitive sports or it can be turned into a symphony concert hall by increasing the seating to 2,500 with portable units. A large swimming pool 110 ft long has seating for 450 and is augmented by a smaller 3 ft deep pool for learners. There is a pleasant restaurant, a separate catering area for parties of 160, snack-bar facilities for 600 and licensed bars. In addition there are strategically sited vending machines for hot and cold drinks.

"The theatre is an integral part of the whole, sharing the common entrance, foyer, restaurant, bars and toilets, an important factor in the costing. It was stated that this

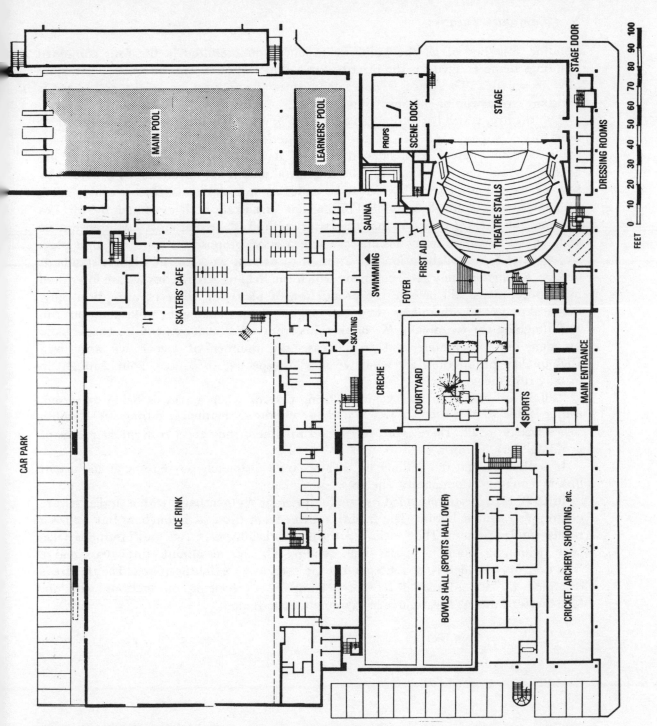

Fig. 1   Plan of Billingham Forum showing the various recreational activities provided for. Theatre at bottom right. (Architects: Elder Lester and Partners, Middlesbrough) (TABS Magazine)

bonding together of all the buildings in one group resulted in the four combined buildings being erected for the price of three detached ones. This integration has other obvious virtues. The place is open daily from 7 a.m. until midnight and there is constant circulation of citizens, young and old."

The theatre, which has a total capacity of 675, was never intended to have a resident repertory company and except for a short period in 1968-69 this policy has been adopted. The amateur companies in the area have not used the theatre as they are adequately catered for elsewhere. The stage productions have been mainly provided by touring companies, some of which were under commercial management, others being originated and controlled by the Billingham organization. It is stated by Mr Les Jobson, the theatre director, that the latter method is the one most favoured but he adds that "there are many instances where a good proposition appears (good play, strong cast) for a collaboration. We attempt to present work to the highest standards here in Billingham: any good company which can help us achieve this we are interested in. Future plans still include the production of plays for home consumption only. Classical plays and other plays of educational interest are among them. Productions run at Billingham for two weeks. We book tours from other managements to enable us to broaden our programme and to increase the number of weeks we are 'live.' High-quality productions are what we seek, irrespective of source. Tours brought in usually run one week only.

"Films are shown in the evenings during periods when a play is being rehearsed, during some of the summer weeks and for children's matinées: during 1971, about seven weeks in all. There is no set period for films: they are a convenient means of avoiding 'dark' periods."

It is obvious that this Billingham theatre could ultimately prove to be an important link in a chain of Community Theatres.

In 1972 Manchester provided its satellite town of Wythenshawe with a similar leisure centre, also named Forum. The facilities differ from those at Billingham but follow a rather similar pattern. They include a theatre with 500 seats, two multi-purpose halls, two swimming pools, a sports hall, lending library, restaurant, three bars and a common foyer which is also intended to be used as an exhibition area. The theatre is occupied by a professional repertory company exchanging productions with the Manchester Library Theatre under a common management.

2
What Type of Theatre ?

During the last twenty-five years or so there have been many attempts to break away from old traditions and techniques, to find new, or to rediscover old forms of theatre, forms which it is usual to claim have greater relevance to the social pattern of the second half of this century. There has been a great deal of sporadic experimenting, sometimes rather tentative, often earnestly extravagant and usually dependent on the energy of some enthusiast with the ability to convince others that he has the right answer. Unfortunately (or perhaps fortunately) there are no answers that are incontestably right, although too often matters of doubtful opinion are too readily offered as statements of established fact.

The attempted breakaway is not an exclusively British phenomenon; it appears to be symptomatic of international rebellion against the establishment. Earnest rebels, true to form, "conspire to smash the sorry scheme of things entire" but, equally true to form, offer as replacement a confused selection of heart's desires. In 1967 theatre people from all over the world met in Montreal to discuss—so it was said—Theatre: Why? Theatre: What kind? Theatre: Where and How? Theatre: Form? and the technical and mechanical problems involved. In the event the comment and discussion were so incoherently diffuse that Fred Lebensold, an exasperated American architect of considerable theatre experience, was goaded into a vigorous outburst beginning with "You tell us what you damn well want and we will build it." They didn't.

There was no evidence to suggest that Lebensold's protest created any significant impact. A certain amount of woolly extravagance on the part of those who are able to persuade somebody to pay them for having fun must be accepted as a fact of theatrical life. Cranks create revolutions but there is usually sufficient massive inertia to prevent acceleration from becoming disastrous. Nevertheless, the irresistible force of ardent reform may be able to prove that immovable conservative objects can be nudged just a little in the direction intended—which may be all to the ultimate good.

Alternative Forms of Theatre

There are several popular alternatives to the orthodox proscenium stage and the choice of a theatre form must be an early policy decision as it will affect the whole design of the building. The differences involved are mainly those of relating the stage to the audience and deciding whether the two areas are to share the same architectural space. Each alternative has advantages and disadvantages and each has its enthusiastic advocates who are inclined to exaggerate the virtue of one by comparison with the others. In truth, all are perfectly valid forms of theatre if it is possible to adapt performance to conditions, and if the adaptation is effectively contrived. For our purpose there are conflicting needs and whatever form is favoured it must be practical and suitable.

The Proscenium Stage

This has evolved from the need to make rapid changes of scenery. The height of the stage tower must allow draperies and scenery to be hauled upwards ("flown") out of sight. It must be possible to separate the acting area from the auditorium by means of drapery curtains ("main tabs"): a fireproof wall and a safety curtain must isolate the stage tower from the rest of the building.

Recent changes of fashion in scenic design have reduced the need for flying scenery but demand for the ability to use it dies hard. In numerous halls and small theatres with proscenium stages, although there is no fly-tower (a costly addition), the scenery is nevertheless designed very much as it would be for a stage with flying space. Frustrating inconvenience can be avoided if the designs are based on the actual conditions.

In the theatres built during the nineteenth and early twentieth centuries it was usual to emphasize the proscenium arch by giving it an elaborately decorated frame, hence the term "picture-frame stage," used scornfully by advocates of alternatives but often rather affectionately by non-advocates. Current architectural practice is to omit the emphatic frame and for the opening to be bordered by the side walls and ceiling of the auditorium. On each side of the proscenium opening and at the rear of the acting area there must be space for scenic backings to doors and windows, for the packing of scenery and properties required in different scenes and for the accommodation of actors about to make an entrance or after making an exit. In such theatres the whole audience must sit facing the proscenium opening and, as in any form of theatre, should be able to see the whole of the floor of the acting area, a requirement more honoured in the breach than in the observance.

The Open End-stage

As the name implies, the stage is at one end of the auditorium, the audience facing it as with the proscenium stage. The end-stage extends over the full area between the side walls, as in a concert hall. Movable scenery may or may not be used. There would not usually be any fly-tower, although flying facilities are sometimes demanded even for this type of theatre. Changes of scenery, if any, are made in full view but in some cases curtains are used to screen the stage during scene-changes. The main difference between end-stage and proscenium stage is that the former has no off-stage space at each side and the stage and auditorium share the same architectural space. The Mermaid Theatre in London is an early modern example. This has a revolve in the stage floor for scene-changes.

The Thrust Stage

This modern adaptation of the Greco-Roman theatre is probably the most popular of the open stages. In its basic form the audience encloses the stage within an arc of something like 180°. Its current popularity is largely due to the influence of the late Tyrone Guthrie and Tanya Moiseiwitsch, who were mainly responsible for the design of the Festival Theatre at Stratford, Ontario, in 1953. They also collaborated when the Tyrone Guthrie Theatre was built ten years later in Minneapolis, USA. These theatres have influenced design in many parts of the world. The audience in this type of theatre should be distributed more or less equally within an arc around a peninsular stage; in the Minneapolis version the layout is asymmetric, the object being to dissuade the customers from assuming (not without some justification) that the centre block of seats was likely to be the main focus of the acting, which it should not be.

In some theatres there has been a rather futile token adoption of the thrust idea by placing a few seats at each side of the stage. It is a basic requirement that in the production of plays on a thrust stage, as with the central acting area, the pictorial distribution of the actors should differ fundamentally from that on the proscenium and end-stages. On the latter the acting has, of necessity, a front focus, demanding what the late Stephen Joseph called "linear projection," whereas the thrust and centre stages demand multi-directional acting with an inward focus, or in Stephen Joseph's terms, "organic projection." Any scenery used on a thrust stage is limited to providing a background to the acting area, probably creating a number of entrances and acting levels. The background is of limited value to those who occupy the seats towards the ends of the arc. Also, if the stage is a symmetrical arc of 180°, it could become excessively wide in relation to its depth.

Centre Stages

There are two forms, one in which the acting area runs between two opposing tiers of seats, the other having an acting area completely surrounded by the tiers. "Tiers" is important in this context. To give actors and stage staff a free, level access the acting area must not be raised and the seats must therefore be steeply raked to create satisfactory sight-lines. Although scenery is not normally required, properties and lighting are freely used. The audience must see the whole floor of the acting area: the complete pattern created by the actors must be visible. Effective production in this form, with its "organic projection," demands that whichever way the actor turns he shall have as many people behind him as in front, assuming a full house, of course.

To quote Stephen Joseph again: "The main characteristics of the centre stage can be summarized as follows: it is the most radically different form of theatre in terms of acting style from the enclosed theatre: it presents the most extreme extent of audience embrace, i.e. the audience is all round the stage: it thus allows the maximum number of people in the audience to be close to the actors. It breaks the greatest number of today's conventions and thus collects more than its fair share of fanaticism from its supporters and from its detractors."

His latest personal preference (he was never afraid to change his mind) was for a centre-stage theatre having only seven or eight rows of seats, accommodating about 500 people. If that capacity is much exceeded, there could be rather tricky acoustic problems. Amplified speech is not a satisfactory answer: it would contradict the basic principle of this form of theatre, which is the sharing of complete intimacy between audience and actors. Although we are all well conditioned to the use of the disembodied voice it is an anachronism in the playhouse.

Adaptable Theatres

There have been ingenious experiments in the design of theatres in which the layout may be altered at will to suit alternative forms of production. One suspects that adaptability is often demanded because of uncertainty about which particular form is most fashionable at the time. The more revolutionary advocates of adaptability may demand a wide open space in which the acting area and the seating can be pushed around anywhere and anyhow at the whim of the director. These advocates, no doubt, have valid reasons why they should be given such opportunities for having their fun but, as far as one can judge at present, any such demand has little relevance or practicality in the context of the kind of Community Theatre projects we are considering. It could, no doubt, apply to a supplementary experimental studio. Most adaptable theatres are designed with the main, or possibly the sole, purpose of providing for play production. For the type of theatre we are discussing, it is probable that a basically rigid form with some simple flexibility is likely to be the most suitable.

Multi-purpose Theatres

The use of a Community Theatre is very varied and could well include drama, opera, ballet, musicals, revue, pantomime, concerts (orchestral, choral, chamber music, brass band, jazz, pop, folk), poetry readings, film shows, fashion shows, lectures, meetings and conferences.

One of the main problems, of course, is to cater for conflicting acoustic needs. Music and speech demand different conditions which cannot be easily reconciled. Ideally there should be at least two separate auditoriums, but that is an ideal which usually founders on the rock of finance. Also, in most small towns it would be impossible, at the present time, to keep two theatres sufficiently occupied to justify their existence. We have, then, either to abandon the idea or accept some reasonable compromise.

Obviously, a theatre that is large enough to accommodate, say, the Covent Garden Opera or the BBC Symphony Orchestra would not be suitable for the production of *The Kitchen Sink* by the Puddleton Players. The type of theatre we have in mind would not, in any case, expect to book large metropolitan companies. But a theatre designed primarily for drama, with a capacity of 650 or 700, could house quite satisfactorily smaller visiting companies presenting not only plays but also intimate opera and ballet, choral and orchestral concerts, and could also accommodate the local amateur operatic and dramatic societies. The Puddleton Players would probably panic at the idea of selling 700 seats per night. The possibility of being able to reduce the capacity when necessary will be dealt with later.

This need for accommodating a wide variety of performances is not new. In the past it has been the practice to build a comparatively low-cost multi-purpose hall with a flat floor and inadequate stage, it being assumed that provision has thus been made for all or most of the activities mentioned, including bingo and banquets, perhaps, with dancing and all-in wrestling thrown in for good measure and better box-office. For all the purposes likely to be involved, except dancing, banquets and exhibitions, a flat-floored hall is unsuitable: the audience will not be able to see everything they should see. After many years of frustrated argument, persuasive or violent according to mood or provocation, it is at last being generally acknowledged that sight-lines from flat floors are deplorable. If it is decided that a flat floor is absolutely essential, the basic plan will be that of a multi-purpose hall (or possibly, as in America, a "gymnatorium" or "cafetorium"), which must then be converted to a theatre form when required. There are alternative methods of changing the flat-floored hall into a form of temporary theatre:

(a) The floor can be constructed to enable it to be tilted to form a ramp for the seating. The floor would normally rise and fall at the stage end, as shown in Fig. 2. The rake allowed for should be the permitted maximum of 1 in 10. As the height of the stage above the lowest level dictates the possible range of tilt, it will be found that even with a maximum stage height of 3 ft 6in. $(1 \cdot 1$ m$)$[1] a rake of 1 in 10 would restrict the length of the tilting floor to about 35 ft (10·6m). In that case, any additional seating required could be at the rear on permanent or retractable tiers. At the stage end there

[1] Since dimensions are in most cases rather approximate, metric equivalents have mostly been rounded off to avoid the misleading appearance of absolute precision that would be given by measurements in metres and millimetres.

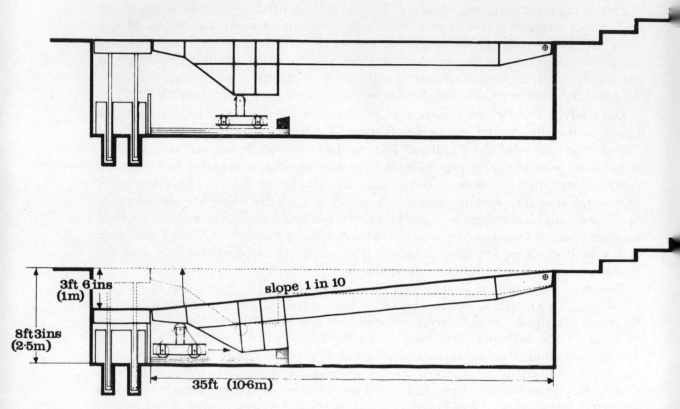

Fig. 2   Section of auditorium floor which can be tilted to create permitted rake of 1 in 10, with lift which when raised provides a common level of auditorium and stage; when lowered, forms a front gangway. (Hall Stage Equipment Ltd)

would be a need for a flat front gangway, and possibly for an orchestra pit. To join the stage to the main floor at a common level it would be necessary to have a movable section which could also form an apron stage. When the apron is removed, the top could provide either the gangway or the orchestra pit floor. Fig. 3 shows this apron with a retractable understructure.

Any such tilting floor must be included in the initial planning as space must be provided for the mechanism below floor-level. The planning of entrances and exits must also allow for any adjustment to the varying levels.

(*b*) Retractable tiered platforms (bleachers) may be fitted to a rigid flat floor, so designed that the height of the risers is related to the stage height to provide good sight-lines. When retracted, the tiers would occupy a space of something like 5 ft (1·5 m) in depth. They could be fitted with folding seats, which would save time and

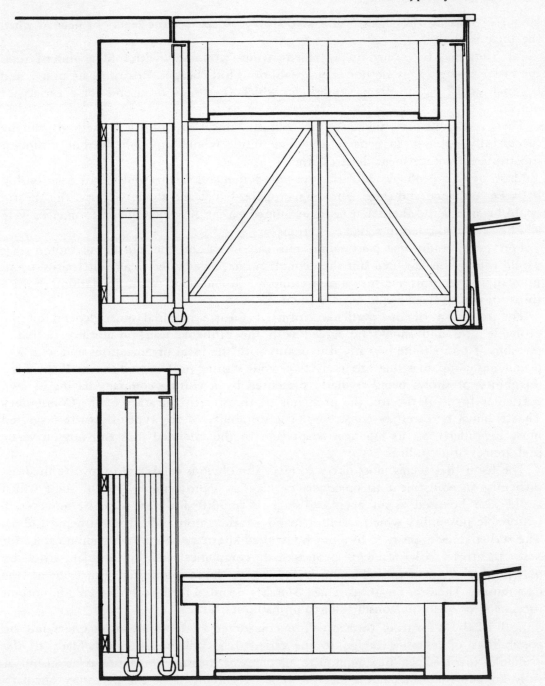

Fig. 3 *Stage extension with retractable understructure and removable top which may be used as floor or front gangway. Alternative to lift in Fig. 2. (Rank Strand Electric Ltd)*

labour in making the changes and save storage space for the seats not needed when the floor is clear.

(*c*) Tiers may be formed by portable rostrums, preferably with folding under-frames for easier storage. This method is more laborious but cheaper. Rostrums are best suited to small areas, e.g. in drama studios, in which they may be useful for a variety of purposes.

There are limits to the sizes of halls in which any of these methods can be successfully applied. In general, the final result would probably be but a modest substitute for a permanent theatre form.

Most of the probable activities suggested demand a theatre-type of relationship between audience and stage. For drama, opera, ballet and some concerts, the theatre could be any of the alternative types examined earlier, provided the performances were all effectively adapted to actual conditions.

For revue, traditional pantomime, musical shows and the like a proscenium stage would usually be favoured but they could, in fact, be adapted to any alternative form. Film shows, lectures and meetings presuppose an end-stage form. For fashion shows a thrust or centre stage would be very suitable.

The selection of the particular form of theatre required must depend on the probable uses and should be agreed with the probable users in advance if that is possible. There should be early discussions with the local organizations and with any producing companies that are likely to provide visiting professional shows. If there is a possibility of shows being regularly presented by a visiting company having its own particular form of theatre, the problems of transfer to the stage of the Community Theatre must be carefully considered. The suitability of any type of theatre suggested must be judged on its practical adaptation to the intended uses and not on vague preferences or prejudices.

The form that seems most likely to meet the obvious needs and to involve the least difficulty in adjustment to preconceived ideas is a proscenium type of stage which could also be used as an open end-stage. A modified thrust stage is, however, a reasonable possibility which would demand a rather more radical adjustment of ideas. The thrust stage appears to be a much favoured alternative to the proscenium stage for new theatres with resident professional companies and, if regular visits by play-producing professional companies are to be an essential function of the Community Theatre, the thrust stage, suitably adapted to the other equally important uses, must be seriously considered as a probable starter.

Both of these forms of theatre will be considered in the following chapters and the possibilities of adapting design to the varied usage will be examined. Many of the principles involved will be common to all types of theatre. The actual relationship of stage to audience does not affect the basic requirements of the necessary ancillary accommodation.

3
The Auditorium

That most theatres exist for the sale of entertainment is a fact that may be strongly disputed by those earnest people who would have the theatre revered as a temple of art, fostering the cultural well-being of the community. It may have this virtue on the side but it is basically a shop selling either a commodity that may attract a small discriminating minority or one that has a wide and catholic appeal. To exist in our present society it has to attract customers who will pay good money for what is offered for sale, even though it may be necessary for the community to subsidize the product if it is thought to be impossible to charge an economic price based on actual costs. No matter what may be the price and quality of the goods offered, however, they must now be presented in attractive surroundings to customers who are justifiably becoming more choosey.

Hundreds of scruffy, uncomfortable Victorian theatres failed to survive the first onslaught of competition from the movies, not solely because of novelty and differences in entertainment value but also because of the much higher standards of comfort offered by the cinemas. One has heard it suggested by an eminent theatre director, who should know better, that there is merit in making theatre audiences slightly uncomfortable. This is a nonsensical exaggeration: seats can be comfortable enough to encourage relaxation without inducing somnolence. Audiences can and do adopt the effective sanction of staying away from uncomfortable theatres. In any case, it is a poor performance that cannot keep a comfortably seated audience alert. Any new theatre must be pleasing and comfortable if it is to attract more than the stoical few who will continue to endure penitential discomfort, appalling sight-lines and drab surroundings in order to witness a live show. There is a large untapped market for live entertainment well presented and energetically sold. Any Community Theatre's productions must be publicized with vigour if it is to be successful.

Seating Capacity

The theatre in Britain has become accustomed to small audiences and because subsidies can often offset operational losses some theatre people are too ready to underestimate the seating capacities required. In the USA where they are less inclined towards modesty of size, it is not unusual to find theatres (which would be called auditoriums) for varied usage in schools, colleges and communities, with seating capacities of 1500 and more; for theatres intended to attract professional tours a capacity of 2000 is stated to be the minimum. These sizes would be daunting to equivalent British organizations, with some justification.

The selection of a suitable seating capacity can create the most difficult problem to be solved before a Community Theatre can be planned. There are usually wide differences in the capacities estimated by the people concerned.

In 1967 a Committee appointed jointly by the National Operatic and Dramatic Association and the British Drama League conducted a survey through their area representatives in all parts of the United Kingdom. The following is a summary of the seating capacities suggested for a Community Theatre.

Amateur Operatic Societies		*Amateur Dramatic Societies*	
Under 500	15%	150/300	39%
500/750	30%	400/600	50%
750/1000	25%	Over 600	5%
Over 1000	10%	Not stated	6%
Not stated	20%		
	45·5% favoured capacities of 500 to 850		

A similar variety of suggestions would be offered by those interested in non-theatrical performances, particularly if they have hitherto attracted only small audiences, probably in buildings with minimum facilities and amenities. The maximum capacity available will to some extent determine the type and quality of professional shows that could be booked. A new and attractive theatre should increase audience appeal but it would be uneconomic to provide a maximum capacity that would be needed only very rarely.

From the estimates quoted it seems likely that a capacity of about 700 should meet the needs of most amateur operatic societies, although some of them may have to consider giving more performances or have the pleasure of exhibiting "House Full" notices every night instead of on Saturday only.

A capacity of 700 should be suitable for small but first-class professional companies. Quite obviously it would be rejected by star-studded companies of National Theatre standards. The prestige companies could, however, organize secondary touring companies, geared in composition and cost to the Community Theatres circuit. A capacity of 700 would be too large for most amateur societies presenting plays and methods of reducing the capacity when necessary to something like 400 should be considered. In a theatre of this size there should not be any serious acoustic problems in planning for the suggested varied use of the theatre.

The agreed maximum capacity will determine whether the audience can be accommodated on one tiered floor or whether a balcony should be included. If a balcony is required it may be thought necessary to ramp the ground floor, to limit the total height of the building. The maximum slope allowed is 1 in 10: the sight-lines are not perfect but it may be a permissible compromise.

If variable capacity is a requirement the auditorium must be designed to allow for isolation or removal of those seats not required without destroying the intimacy of the theatre. Intimacy does not necessarily mean limited spaciousness: a well-designed and well-filled auditorium with a thousand seats may be more intimate than one with smaller capacity in which there are wide-open spaces and fragmented distribution of seats. It is bad practice to have blocks of seats that must be left unoccupied, unless they can be effectively screened. Anybody with experience of acting or of public speaking knows that a closely knit audience takes on a collective personality. If the audience is thinly scattered or there are large empty spaces, there is loss of collective reaction. This may be a good argument in favour of selling all seats at the same price if vision and acoustics are good in every part of the auditorium, a democratic virtue that would have an added bonus in simplicity of booking. If variable capacity depends on some of the seats being portable there should be simple means of moving and storing them quickly.

It is now generally agreed by theatre planners that no member of the audience should be more than about 70 ft (22 m) from the setting-line on the stage, which would normally imply about 65 ft (20 m) from the front edge. These limits are appropriate to play performances but are less so to musical shows for which a limit of 100 ft (30 m) is acceptable. Whatever the type of performance, however, seeing and hearing will deteriorate if the distance from the performer exceeds the limits suggested. One must not be misled by these limits: if the stage is very wide there could be excessive diagonal views from the side seats to the opposite side of the stage, or across the thrust or centre stage. These sight-lines must be carefully plotted.

The size of the theatre is affected by the arm-to-arm width of the seats as well as their total number, and also by the unobstructed vertical space (seatway) between the rows. The seatway will dictate the permitted maximum distance from a gangway and the number of gangways required will affect the overall size and layout of the auditorium. These problems and their alternative solutions are examined in detail in *Theatre Planning* (see Book List): this should be carefully studied.

Although the spacing between rows is a major factor in designing the layout, the seatway is the vital measurement affecting safety regulations. Subject to these regulations, the layout should be designed to give maximum concentration of the audience: to meet the safety requirements it may be necessary to have a centre gangway which would, of course, occupy some of the best viewing positions. There are times, however, when a centre gangway can provide an effective entrance for actors; such a gangway should not be regarded as a total loss if it has to be provided.

The possibility of having "continental seating" may be considered. This is the term used for seating in which the rows are continuous: the lack of intersecting gangways, splitting the audience into groups, has advantages but excessively long rows can create disastrous opportunities for late-comers, whose trail of chaos almost always extends to centre seats.

Whatever layout is adopted and however strong may be the temptation to fit the maximum number of seats into the minimum space, the old practice of allowing only the minimum seatway should be avoided. All members of the audience, even those with long legs, are entitled to reasonable comfort; it is antisocial and bad business to ignore the fact.

Sight-lines

From any seat in the house there should be an uninterrupted view of the whole floor of the acting area over the heads of the people in front. Of course, heads will be at different heights and it is not possible to plan for the small person who is unlucky enough to have booked a seat immediately behind the one occupied by the tallest person in the house. The average eye-line of a seated person is accepted, for planning purposes, as 3 ft 8 in. (1·1 m) and the top of the head is assumed to be 4 in. (0·100 mm) higher. The sight-lines are plotted by relating these arbitrary measurements to (*a*) height of stage; (*b*) height of each row of seats; and (*c*) distance between rows. It follows that the lower the stage, the greater must be the rake of the auditorium. In plotting the sight-lines it will be found that with a uniform height of risers the sight-lines deteriorate slightly as the distance from the stage increases and it is desirable to fix the first visible point on the stage floor from the rear seats. That point would be the normal setting line, but if the acting area is to be extended on occasion by a movable apron stage the sight-lines must be adjusted to the front of the apron. If there are cross gangways there must be allowance for the effect on the sight-lines from the seats beyond the gangway. The row immediately beyond the cross gangway should be raised sufficiently to allow for the extra width between it and the row in front.

There is a current fashion for having stages as low as possible. This means that the seating tiers must have maximum rake, thereby increasing the total height and the cost of the building, with dubious justification. As the maximum height of the stage must be below the theoretical eye-line of 3 ft 8 in. (1·1 m) it should not exceed 3 ft 6 in. (1·07 m). A lower stage would be more acceptable to the occupants of the front rows; but unless the rake of the auditorium can be increased proportionately, concern for the front rows must not override the needs of the majority. The rake of the auditorium also affects the lateral sight-lines. If the heads of the people in front are below the line of vision there is no problem, provided the total width occupied by seats is properly related to the acting area. If the view is obstructed because the rake of the seating is insufficient for the height of the stage, some relief, though very marginal, is possible if the seats are staggered so that the people behind may have that extra but rather restricted angle of vision over the shoulders of those in front; this is no justifiable substitute for good sight-lines. The vertical sight-lines are particularly important if there is a balcony and/or a proscenium arch. These are discussed later (see page 34).

Auditorium Ceiling

Gone are the days when a theatre's ceiling had to be an exhibit of the plasterer's art, supporting impressive chandeliers. Inflated costs and functional aesthetics are not solely responsible for loss of this former opulence. However effectively sight-lines are planned, they depend basically on light, without which there is no vision. The quality of vision is affected by the direction, dispersal and intensity of the light and, as much of the acting area can be effectively lit only from positions within the auditorium space, ceiling positions are needed for the ever increasing number of lanterns claimed to be necessary in modern stage lighting practice. There must be safe and easy access for those whose job it is to focus the lanterns, change the lamps and colour filters and, if the spirit moves them (or the stage manager is forcibly persuasive), to clean the lenses and reflectors. From these positions, which must be carefully planned as an integral part of the structure, it must be possible to direct light to any part of the acting area. It happens far too often that, because of errors in the siting or construction of lighting bridges, the lanterns have been forced into positions which made focusing and maintenance a hazardous and painful exercise of inhuman dexterity.

How far the architect is able to combine his aesthetics with the effective siting of equipment for lighting, air conditioning, electrical wiring, etc., is his problem. He may decide to omit any suspended ceiling and either to reveal the structural splendour of the roof trusses and lighting bridges, or to obscure them by use of down-light "blinders." Whatever the decision, there must be co-operation with the specialist suppliers and conflicting demands must be satisfactorily settled.

For each of the differing types of open stage there are different problems in the siting of lighting equipment. For a proscenium stage the siting is less complicated: apertures for the lighting are more or less parallel to the front edge of the stage. It is quite usual practice to allow a sloping ceiling, or a suspended ceiling panel, to form the proscenium head, preferably with a lighting aperture immediately in front of the acting area. For such a theatre that has no fly-tower, there is something to be said for continuing the ceiling panel arrangement over the acting area. That something is said later (see page 37).

The ceiling area should not reflect light from the stage into the auditorium. Any highlight on a strongly reflective surface is distracting. Vision depends on contrasts of light and shade, which are dominated by the strongest visible light. Consequently, an unwanted highlight on a ceiling or border, or on the proscenium edges, will make the acting area appear to be underlit, an illusion that is at once removed if the intrusive light is killed.

Acoustics

In a Community Theatre used for the various purposes suggested there will be some conflict in the required control of reflection and absorption of the varied sounds. In a theatre of limited size the problems are not acute but the advice of an acoustic consultant is desirable. The structural conditions must not make it necessary to use amplified speech. For stage performances generally and for drama particularly, the direct voice is a vital asset. In spite of progressive improvements in the quality of amplified sound, that quality is so easily and so often distorted by insensitive control. Of course, amplified sound must be available for those performers to whom microphones and maximum decibels are indispensable to their peculiar popular trade. It is also necessary to relay music and "noises off" that may be incidental to production.

Insulation against external noise is important. It is disastrous when a quietly dramatic scene is shattered by the aggressive exhaust of a passing motor-cycle or by the steady hum from a badly sited ventilation system.

Auditorium Décor

As an audience enters a theatre the first impression should be stimulating and pleasurable. Colours that are dull and drab, or clinically cold, should be avoided. Brightness and light are needed; but not too much light. If the auditorium is too brightly lit the eyes will not be conditioned for the intended effect of the acting area lighting when the curtain rises. Smooth dimming of the auditorium lights helps the transition, but transition must not be too steep.

To avoid excessive reflection of light from walls and ceilings there is a temptation to paint them black, which can be depressingly funereal when the house lights are on. Dark blue can be more effective, with house lights on or off. An alternative is to rely on the basic texture of unpainted brick walls, a method used effectively in the University Theatre, Manchester, and the Thorndike Theatre, Leatherhead. Seats upholstered in a variety of colours can give an air of attractive gaiety, as in the Guthrie Theatre, Minneapolis.

The general scheme of decoration should be designed for its effect when the auditorium is practically empty as well as when it is completely full and not only when it is fully lit but also when the house lights are dimmed. When the lights are on, the environment must be pleasing and comfortable; when they are off and the stage is lit, the environment should fade out of conscious vision.

4
The Stage

In any form of theatre the size and shape of the acting area, i.e. the area of the stage visible to the audience, will largely determine the layout of the auditorium. Experience has shown that the acting areas of Thrust and Centre stages should be smaller than those of the Proscenium and End stages. Alfred Emmet, director of the Questors Theatre, Ealing, states that when working on Thrust and Centre stages "practically every square foot of floor space can be used at any time. This is far from being the case on a proscenium stage where one has to string the actors across the stage in such a way that probably quite half of even a deep stage is liable to be masked or otherwise unusable at one given moment." He also states that "a crowd of thirty or forty looked very thin and inadequate on the Questors' open stage of about 460 sq ft." (*TABS*, Vol. 25, No. 1.) One knows, from experience, that a crowd of half that number can suggest considerably more on a proscenium stage of similar size.

Proscenium Opening: Width

Opinions about the maximum width of a proscenium arch will vary considerably, even though the people involved have a common experience and comparable expertise. Up to about twenty years ago it was generally agreed that for play production, particularly by amateurs, an opening of about 28 ft (8·5 m) was a sensible maximum. Since then quite a lot of new theatres have been built and quite a lot of ideas have changed.

It is interesting to compare the nineteenth-century Lyric Theatre, Hammersmith (Fig. 4(*a*)), with the 1969 Thorndike Theatre, Leatherhead (Fig. 4(*b*)). One need not compare the Victorian opulence of the Lyric proscenium arch (a gem of a "picture frame") with the functional restraint of the Thorndike: for our purpose the difference is that the Lyric, with a proscenium opening of 24 ft (7·3 m) has a capacity of 500 in the stalls and dress circle (ignoring the gallery), whereas the Thorndike, with a proscenium opening of 36 ft (11 m) seats 530 on one tiered level, with more liberal spacing. In each case the maximum plan distance from the stage does not exceed 60 ft (18·3 m). Because there is a gallery, the height of the Lyric's decorative ceiling over the stalls is 36 ft (11 m) compared with a maximum of about 20 ft (6 m) to the sloped ceiling of the Thorndike.

Fig. 4(a) Decorative proscenium of the Lyric Theatre, Hammersmith (1895). (By courtesy of the Director-General, Greater London Council)

Fig. 4(b) The Thorndike Theatre, Leatherhead (1969) illustrating modern type of proscenium. (Architect: Roderick Ham ARIBA)

It is also interesting to study the relationship of seating capacity to width of proscenium in the following new theatres in Britain:

Proscenium Stages	Width of Prosc.	No. of seats
Gateway, Chester	32 ft (9·8 m)	500 (19 rows)
Playhouse, Nottingham	32 ft (9·8 m)	756 (two tiers)
Ad. Genée, East Grinstead	34 ft (10·4 m)	330 (15 rows)
Little, Newport (Mon)	36 ft (11 m)	410 (adaptable)
Thorndike, Leatherhead	36 ft (11 m)	530 (16 rows)
Shaw, Camden	40 ft (12·2 m)	510 (13 rows)
Congress, Eastbourne	45 ft (13·7 m)	1678 (two tiers)

End Stages without Proscenium		
Mermaid, London	48 ft (14·6 m)	499 (19 rows)
Crescent, Birmingham	55 ft (16·8 m)	288 (adaptable)

There is a reasonably consistent relationship of width of proscenium opening to number and distribution of seats, a relationship not found in the following selection of Victorian theatres (some of them no longer existing), taken at random from the *Stage Guide* of 1946. Of course these theatres may have had two or three balconies and the spacing of the rows and seats would usually be cramped by modern standards. From many of the side seats and those in the galleries in theatres of this period the sight-lines were pretty bad.

	Width of Prosc.	No. of seats
Lyric, Hammersmith	24 ft (7·3 m)	755
Whitehall, London	27 ft 6 in (8·4 m)	619
Royalty, Chester	28 ft (8·5 m)	956
Grand, Derby	30 ft (9·1 m)	1435
King's, Edinburgh	32 ft (9·8 m)	1950*
Grand, Leeds	33 ft (10 m)	1531
Palace, London	33 ft 9 in (10·3 m)	824
Drury Lane, London	42 ft 6 in (13 m)	2238

*According to the *Stage Guide*, distribution of the 1950 seats was: Stalls 626, Dress Circle 294, Upper Circle 308, Gallery 650, Boxes 72. As a playgoer who served a compressed apprenticeship in similar galleries I accept 650 as typical.

Discussion of this relationship of proscenium opening to total seating capacity has provoked my collaborator, Robert Adams to resolve the problems in terms of diagrams, graphs and tables (see Figs. 5, 6, 7 and 8). He uses as a basis a conventional proscenium theatre with the alternative of continental seating to the more usual blocks separated by a centre aisle. He has assumed an inward splay of 10° at each side of the stage scenery: this is sufficiently usual to be justified. The object is to show the maximum number of seats permitted if every member of the audience is to be able to see the entire width of the acting area, nobody being more than 70 ft distant from the setting-line. The capacity is substantially affected by the angle of sight from the point 70 ft (21 m), i.e. whether the line is to near, centre or far side of the stage. The distance between the rows of seats and arm-to-arm width are important factors. The data given should be accepted as a rough-and-ready-reckoner for use during initial consideration. Any of the possible deviations from the assumed measurements could affect the result in the detailed planning.

Frederick Bentham, a vigorous opponent of the wide opening, states in *New Theatres in Britain:* "The biggest objection to the large opening is the cost of scenery to fill the space behind and the proscenium stage is nothing if it is not a scenic stage. It should be realized that an opening of 40 ft (12·2 m) is virtually the same as that at the Royal Opera House, Covent Garden, or the Theatre Royal, Drury Lane. This can take a lot of scenery and there will be constant budget trouble over this and extras to crowd these wide open spaces when necessary. On the other hand if a wide stage is framed in, then the theatre will not look right, the stage does not belong and it will in any case represent so much idle space most of the time. A proscenium opening is as large as it is made to look rather than as large as it is, and the 30 ft (9·1 m) plus or minus a little commonly found in London's West End takes both musicals and straight drama in its stride."

It is true that if representational scenery is used on a wide stage in the old conventional manner, a lot of scenery may be necessary but it is quite often shown that well-designed suggestive scenery can be very much less. Even for an orthodox interior set we are not compelled to have a box of three walls with its rear "Centre-opening" leading to the inevitable garden balustrade beyond. Fig. 9 shows that for a simple box set designed for a 24 ft (7·3 m) opening, the scenic flats could have a plan run of something like 54 ft (16·5 m), creating an acting area of about 390 sq ft (36·2 m²). The setting has the splay of about 10° inwards from the proscenium edge previously referred to. Fig. 10 shows that a similar set for an opening of 40 ft (12·2 m) would need a 69 ft (21 m) run of flats giving an acting area of about 650 sq ft (60·4 m²). A more effective triangular setting for such an opening could, however, reduce the run of flats to 54 ft (16·5 m) and the acting area to about 420 sq ft (39 m²): there would also be fewer masking problems in plotting the actors' moves.

If an invisible fourth wall is acceptable there is no good reason why a third wall should not also be invisible (see Fig. 11). Actually, the shape of the setting and size of

Text contd. on page 33.

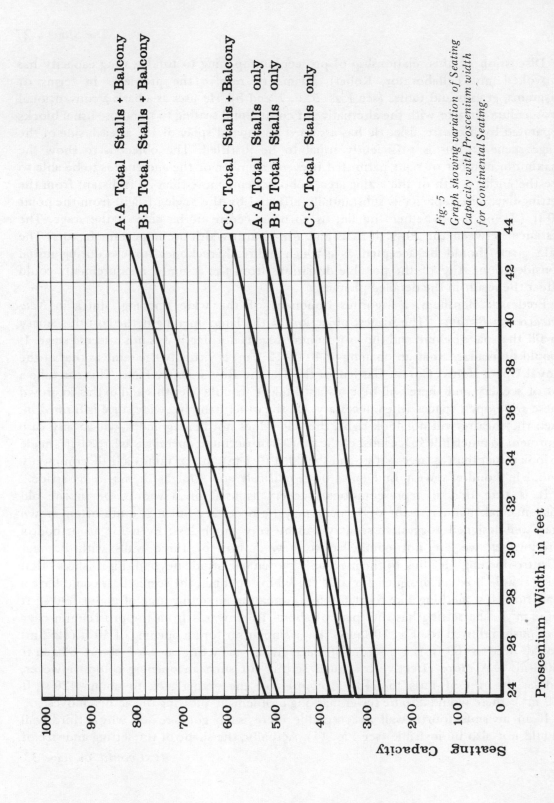

A·A Total Stalls + Balcony
B·B Total Stalls + Balcony

C·C Total Stalls + Balcony

A·A Total Stalls only
B·B Total Stalls only

C·C Total Stalls only

Proscenium Width in feet

Seating Capacity

Fig. 5
Graph showing variation of Seating
Capacity with Proscenium width
for Continental Seating.

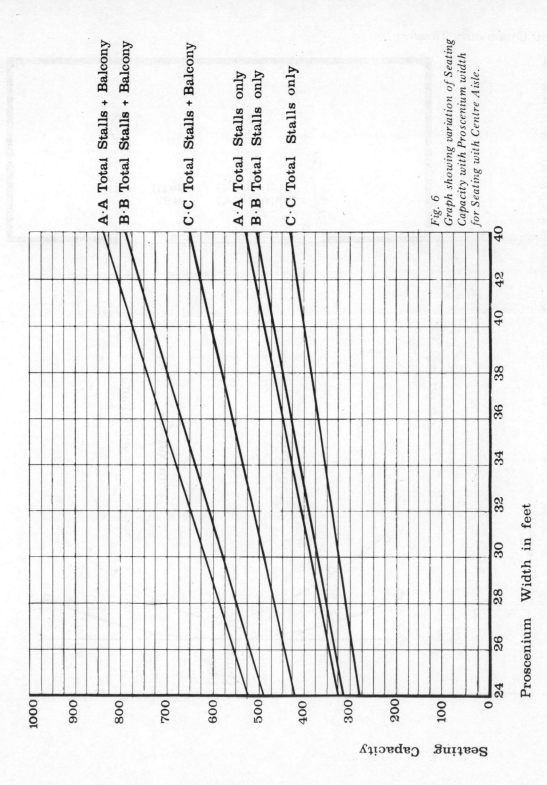

A·A Total Stalls + Balcony
B·B Total Stalls + Balcony

C·C Total Stalls + Balcony

A·A Total Stalls only
B·B Total Stalls only

C·C Total Stalls only

Fig. 6
Graph showing variation of Seating Capacity with Proscenium width for Seating with Centre Aisle.

Proscenium Width in feet

Seating Capacity

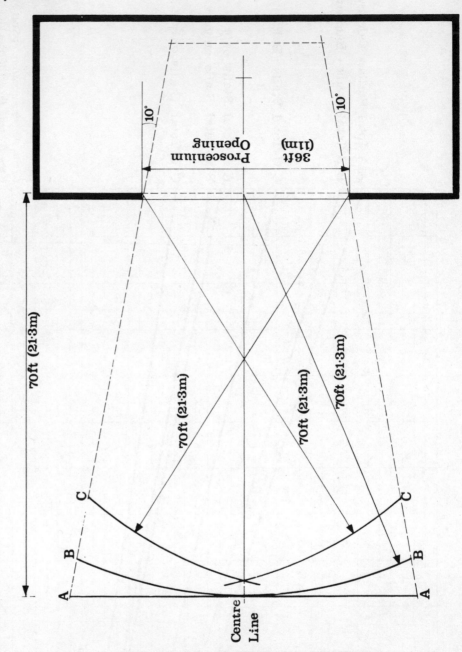

Fig. 7 *Plan showing limitation of sight-lines by restricting seating distance to 70 ft (21·3 m), either to centre line or to further edge of stage.*

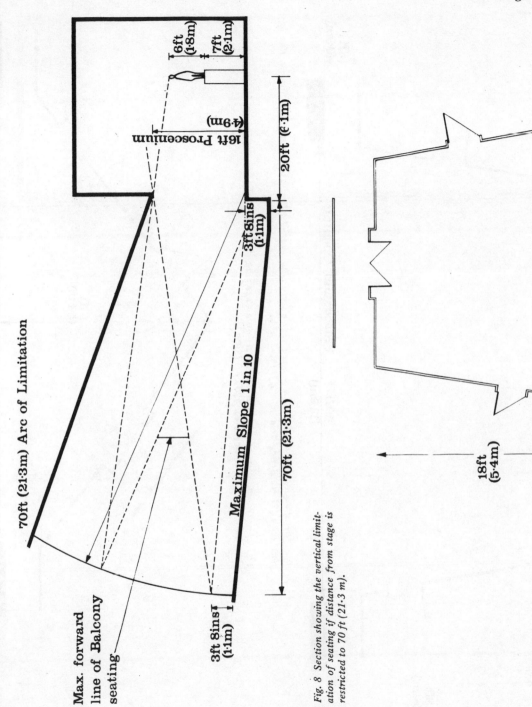

70ft (21·3m) Arc of Limitation

Max. forward
line of Balcony
seating

Maximum Slope 1 in 10

70ft (21·3m)

3ft 8ins
(1·1m)

3ft 8ins
(1·1m)

16ft Proscenium (4·9m)

20ft (6·1m)

6ft
(1·8m)

7ft
(2·1m)

Fig. 8 *Section showing the vertical limitation of seating if distance from stage is
restricted to 70 ft (21·3 m).*

3ft (0·9m)

24ft (7·3m)

18ft
(5·4m)

Fig. 9 *Ground-plan of an orthodox box-
set on a stage with 24 ft (7·3 m) wide
proscenium opening. Run of flats: 54 ft
(16·5 m). Acting Area: 390 sq ft
(36·2 m²)*

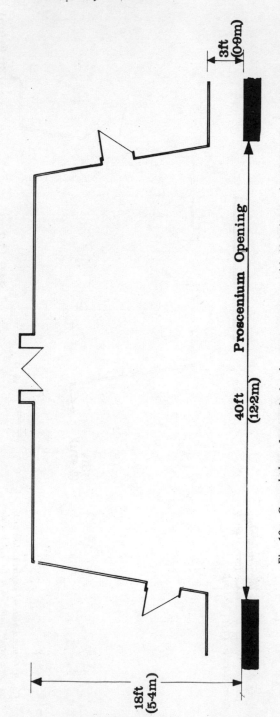

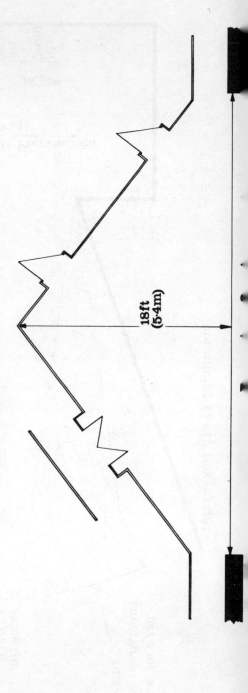

Fig. 10   Ground-plan of an orthodox box-set on a stage with 40 ft (12·2 m) wide proscenium opening. Run of flats: 69 ft (21 m). Acting Area: 650 sq ft (60·4 m²).

Fig. 11   Ground-plan of triangular interior set on a stage with 40 ft (12·2 m) wide proscenium opening. Run of flats: 54 ft (16·5 m). Acting Area: 420 sq ft (39 m²).

the acting area could be varied without destroying the idea. This is not to argue that a 40 ft (12 m) opening is desirable: one would argue, however, that there need not be the dire consequences feared if sight-lines dictate that the stage opening has to be wider than 30 ft (9 m): as Bentham says, the "proscenium opening is as large as it is made to look." It cuts both ways. For large read small!

Width of opening, total capacity and layout of auditorium are interdependent. Good sight-lines must not be sacrificed to inhibitions about the width of the acting area but there must be a nice balance between the number and overall width of the seating rows so that good sight-lines and an opening of sensible width result. To keep the proscenium width down to a reasonable size it may be necessary to include a balcony. Omission of a balcony in the Birmingham Repertory Theatre of 900 seats (opened in 1971) has resulted in there being a proscenium opening with a width of 50 ft (15·2 m), which is distressingly excessive by any standard. It is quite true, as Bentham has suggested, that reduction of the width by means of movable screens or by an inner false proscenium, is not a good idea. Sight-lines from the side seats would be ruined and the framed-picture effect would be emphasized. Deterioration of sight-lines from the side seats in the front rows is shown in Fig. 12. Of course, there is some improvement as the distance from the stage increases.

Fig. 12   Plan showing extent of deterioration of sight-lines if width of proscenium opening is reduced by one-fifth.

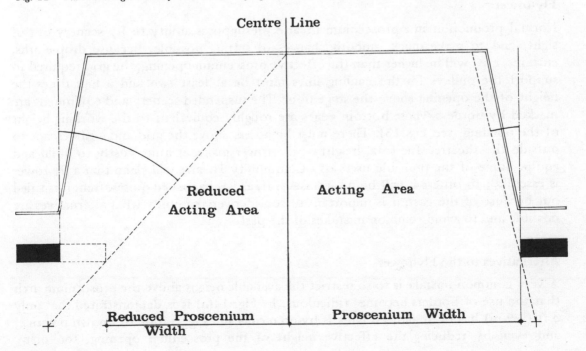

Proscenium Opening: Height

The height should be reasonably proportionate to the width but the architectural height is not necessarily the working height. Although the dominant proscenium arch of the Victorian theatre was very high, the effective opening was almost always cut down to something like 18 ft (5·5 m) by a decorative pelmet and/or a border inside the arch, known as a proscenium border. This is clearly shown in the Lyric Theatre illustration (Fig. 4(a)). 18 ft (5·5 m) is a popular standard height of scenic flats in professional theatres. On amateur stages the flats may vary from 10 ft (3 m) to 16 ft (4·9 m). It has been customary for pelmets and proscenium borders to be used because the permanent arch was designed primarily for its auditorium effect and not for its stage function.

The effective height of the opening will put a limit to the vertical sight-lines, which will be most critical from the highest seats in the house and from those underneath the balcony, if any. It should be possible to see from every seat an actor who may be standing on a 7 ft (2·1 m) high rostrum (allowing for a possible entrance below) at the rear of the acting area, say 18 ft (5·5 m) to 20 ft (6·1 m) up-stage. No matter how well the sight-lines have been planned theoretically for the architectural opening, it is the ultimate working height of the opening that really matters to the sight-lines. This height also affects the positions and the efficiency of the FOH lighting equipment.

Fly-tower

Normal production in a proscenium theatre presupposes ability to fly scenery out of sight, and to make quick, smooth changes of setting possible. Because drop-cloths, curtains, etc., will be higher than the effective proscenium opening, the grid required to support the pulleys for the hauling lines must be at least two and a half times the height of the opening above the stage floor. The suspended scenery and equipment are masked by borders whose bottom edges are roughly equivalent to the working height of the opening (see Fig. 13). There must be access above the grid and a fire-escape to outside the theatre. The total height of the tower makes it quite costly to build and equip. Some of the probable users of a Community Theatre will claim that a fly-tower is essential: to others it will be unnecessary. If, as has happened quite often, it is ruled out because of the cost, it is important to consider very carefully what alternatives are possible and to avoid common mistakes of the past.

Alternatives to the Fly-tower

A very common mistake is to so restrict the available height above the proscenium arch that the use of borders becomes ridiculous. In Fig. 14(a) it is demonstrated that only 3 ft (0·9 m) has been allowed (this is by no means an exaggeration of known practice) and even by reducing the effective height of the proscenium opening, too many

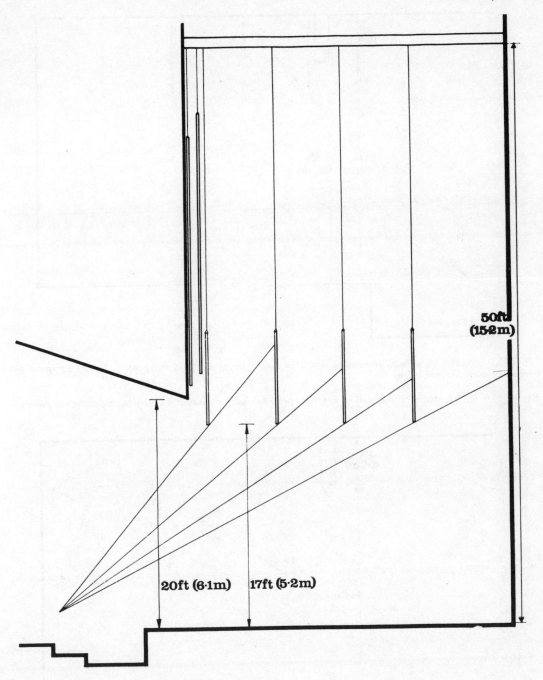

50ft
(15·2 m)

20ft (6·1m)   17ft (5·2m)

Fig. 13   Section showing reduction of the effective height of a proscenium opening by a typical use of borders.

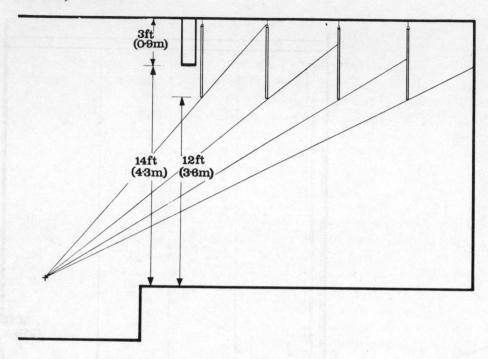

Fig. 14(a)   Section of a small stage with restricted height above proscenium opening showing a typical use of borders to provide extra height.

Fig. 14(b)   An alternative use of ceiling panels to provide masking without reducing the height of the proscenium opening.

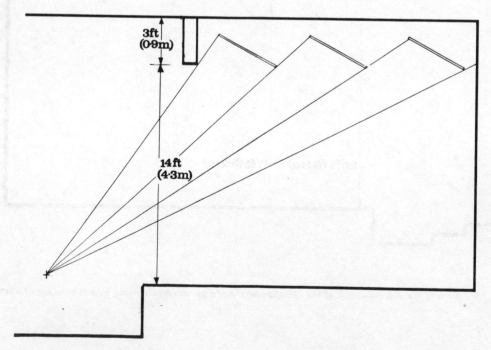

borders are necessary to mask whatever equipment is suspended and there is not enough space between the borders to allow for satisfactory lighting. In the past some of us have argued that there should be at least 8 ft (2·4 m) above the opening to allow the number of borders to be reduced and possibly to permit slight adjustment of their height and that of any other suspended equipment. It is, however, more sensible to recognize that although borders are necessary if there is a fly-tower, on stages where there is not adequate flying space borders should be made superfluous. They obstruct the lighting, absorb too much sound and can intrude irritatingly into the setting, possibly fouling the tops of scenic flats they are intended to conceal. In what are now very rare cases they can form part of a stage setting, usually an exterior, but this use is not essential. It is suggested, therefore, that if a fly-tower is not to be provided, it is sensible to plan the stage to make borders unnecessary. Fig. 14(*b*) shows how this can be done by the use of ceiling panels. Such panels, constructed like scenic flats, have often been used to replace borders but if the acting area is wide they require suspension points at close intervals to avoid deflection and they can be difficult to move. What is now suggested (see Fig. 15) is that the panels should be constructed as a permanent feature, continuing the line of the auditorium ceiling over the acting area, thus creating what is virtually an end-stage; but it is also suggested that there should be the wing-space facilities of the proscenium stage.

Fig. 15   *Section of stage and auditorium suggesting a common use of ceiling panels; also indicating use of free-standing scenery with curtain backing.*

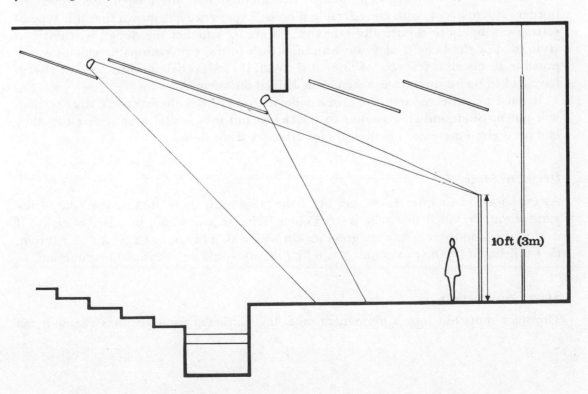

10ft (3m)

For a Community Theatre a stage ceiling of this type has many advantages: the acoustics would be vastly improved for all uses. Adaptation of the stage décor for drama, musical shows, etc., is simple and can be far more effective than the old method of trying to adapt settings to a fly-tower that does not exist.

In the absence of borders, the scenery flats can be placed in any variety of plan arrangements. Drop-cloths can be dispensed with. Cut-out ground-rows, placed in front of a cyclorama background are now more used than conventional back-cloths because they are much cheaper, are more easily moved during scene changes and can, in fact, be more effective pictorially. No matter what may be the structural height of the proscenium opening, it need not be reduced by a pelmet or border. The scenery flats would stand freely in front of a curtain surround (preferably black or dark blue) and need not be more than, say 10 ft (3·1 m) high. By reducing the height of flats below that of the opening, one loses the external scale. A small stage can thus be made to look larger—and a large stage smaller. It is assumed that the acting area would be lit exclusively by spot lanterns making it possible to light the setting from any or all of the overhead positions, leaving the upper space and the curtains unlit. Also, this arrangement makes it easier to use optically projected backgrounds without obstruction: the projector lanterns can be placed in any of the apertures between the ceiling panels. The restricted height of the flats would be more convincing for the average interior set: they would be easier to construct, handle and store, and would cost less than the higher flats that would be dictated by the old method.

This is no revolutionary proposal. The method has often been used, even on border-ridden stages, with considerable success. Experience has shown that this type of setting can be more theatrically effective, no matter whether the design is realistic or stylized. For the benefit of those who may wish to use conventional back-cloths it is possible to install a few sets of lines at the rear, the cloths being rolled, as they always have had to be on such stages when being hauled out of sight.

It must be expected that the people who are fond of the old orthodox stage settings will put up some initial resistance to the change but they would soon realize that they had been given increased possibilities for effective scene design.

Height of Stage

As explained in Chapter 4, the height of the stage must be related to the rake of the auditorium. Provided that rake is steep enough the stage need not be raised at all but if it is raised (and there is no very good reason why it should not be) a height of 3 ft 6 in. (1·1 m) should be the maximum: 2 ft 6 in. (0·8 m) would be a reasonable minimum.

Stage Construction

The stage must not have a permanent rake. If a particular scene requires a ramp it can be provided by movable units. For majority use a raked floor would be a disadvantage. A raked stage does not remedy poor sight-lines created by an inadequately raked auditorium: any difference would be so slight as to be negligible. The raked stage is a legacy from the Georgian theatre in which it served some perspective purpose: that purpose no longer exists as a permanent feature.

Plan Area of Stage

Depth. Although the acting area within a simple interior setting could be quite satisfactory with a depth of about 18 ft (5·5 m) more space would be required for spectacular shows and possibly for other functions staged in a Community Theatre. Beyond the acting area there must be space for backings to doors, arches, etc., for the portable lighting equipment that would be needed in that area, and for the free passage of actors. There should be at least 8 ft (2·4 m) clear space behind the acting area. It is suggested that the total depth from the proscenium curtains to the rear wall should be about 30 ft (9·1 m). In addition, there should be a permanent apron extending about 4 ft (1·2 m) in front of the curtains, preferably with access from the main stage at each side. This apron is a sensible precaution against the possibility of somebody parting the curtains to make an announcement and stepping into a gaping void. The use of a movable extension to the permanent apron will be examined later.

Width. The usual recommendation is that at each side of the stage there should be wing space that is about half the width of the proscenium opening. This is reasonable but arbitrary and if the opening is exceptionally wide the recommendation should not be taken too literally: excessive wing space can be a disadvantage. Flats required for scene changes would be stacked by the side walls and scene-shifters must not be expected to do a marathon run during a quick change.

A few years ago it was rather fashionable to demand space for rolling stages so that a full setting could be assembled in the wings and rolled into position to replace the setting for the previous scene which would have been rolled off at the opposite side. This involved having wing space at each side in excess of the width of the acting area unless expensive lifts were installed to lower the used setting and to raise its replacement. However convenient this may be in the continental opera house, it has never caught on in this country and is, in any case, quite outside the scope of our Community Theatre's needs. Whatever the width of the proscenium opening, the minimum wing space at each side should be about 12 ft (3·7 m); anything less is likely to cause congestion. This space must be left clear of all built-in obstruction: it must be kept free from the clutter of apparatus irrelevant to stage purposes that is so often allowed to intrude because the empty space was so tempting to the planners. Reasonably generous off-stage space at floor-level is of greater importance than the existence of a fly-tower. The stage area is in constant use: flying facilities are far less frequently required and can be sacrificed if the stage settings are suitably designed.

Stage Access

If possible the door leading to the dressing-rooms, etc., can be sited down-stage on the working side, i.e. the side where the stage manager has the prompt-corner. There should also be access from one side of the stage to the other, outside the stage area. Entrances should be as far as possible down-stage, or if necessary up-stage, leaving the maximum amount of side wall space free for the stacking of scenery and properties. If there is a fly-tower with counterweighted lines from the grid, the weight-cradles should have full travel to stage-level (see "Suspension Gear," page 41), otherwise a double-purchase system (more expensive and using double weights) may be necessary. If entrances are provided in the rear wall they should be sited away from the area opposite to the proscenium opening. The back-stage area should have the same floor level as the stage, to avoid steps. Doorways should be about 7 ft (2·1 m) high and 3 ft (0·9 m) wide to allow for actors who may be wearing bulky costumes and high head-dresses. Doors should be self-closing—and silent. Their siting and construction must be agreed with the local fire-precautions authority. There must be large doors for the transfer of scenery and properties from delivery vans to the stage. If at all possible, the relative levels should be so planned that the floors of the vans are likely to be level with the floor of the scene-dock: it is an advantage if the latter can be adjoining but not a part of the actual stage.

There should be direct access from back-stage to front of house, external to both stage and auditorium. Portable stairs which may be placed to give access from the auditorium to the apron stage could be very useful in a Community Theatre.

Apron Stage

It is now fairly common practice to install a lift which will, when raised, extend the apron stage; when lowered it could either extend the seating capacity or could form an orchestra pit. In a Community Theatre this has many advantages. It could create an open stage or platform for use independently or in conjunction with the main stage, either at the same or at a different level. As suggested earlier, there should be access to the apron at each side from the main stage, through entrances in the side walls of the auditorium. Juliet balconies above these entrances can provide raised acting levels and useful positions for lighting equipment. The lift should be as wide as the stage opening: the depth must be decided by its probable uses. It may be an advantage to have two lifts, each say about 6 ft (1·9 m) deep. It would then be possible to have an open stage of 16 ft (4·9 m) deep (including a permanent apron of 4 ft (1·2 m), or, alternatively, one of 10 ft (3 m). The orchestra pit could be similarly varied in size.

If a lift is too expensive, a manually erected structure could be devised. A simple alternative is a retractable understructure with removable top (see Fig. 3, page 15), or an even simpler and less costly alternative would be to use portable rostrums. Much may depend on the availability and the cost of the necessary labour: it is possible that a lift could score for long-term economy. If in doubt, seek advice.

Stage Basement

If a lift is installed there must be access underneath the stage, with appropriate safety precautions, and space should be available for the storage of seats that would not be required when the orchestra pit or the extended apron was in use. It is convenient if these seats are fixed to raked rostrums which can be taken down on the lift and rolled into space underneath the auditorium or the stage.

The basement may, perhaps, provide useful space for stage workshops and stores: also for electrical mains intake, storage batteries for emergency lighting and other apparatus that is better sited away from normal traffic. It is not a good idea to use the basement for combustible materials and, in fact, the fire authorities would probably prohibit such storage. They would, in any case, insist on the whole basement area having maximum fire protection: they should be consulted.

If an orchestra pit is to be used there must be convenient access for players and their instruments to and from the basement; there should also be a "band-room" for their use.

Stage Traps

Although the use of traps in the modern theatre has declined, there are still occasions when one is needed, e.g. Ophelia's grave in *Hamlet*, the cobbler's shop in *Hobson's Choice*, or the Devil's entrance in *Don Juan in Hell* (Act 3, *Man and Superman*). The most useful trap is likely to be a "grave trap" about centre stage and probably measuring 6 x 3 ft (1·8 x 0·9 m). It must be a snug fit and must not squeak at inopportune moments; usefully, but expensively, the top could be an electrically operated slide. If a trap is to be provided, the main joists should run across stage between the side walls to reduce the cutting away.

5
Initial Planning

Whatever form of theatre is chosen, it must be planned to work efficiently. The building of any theatre has its own peculiar problems and unless those responsible for preparing the architect's brief are familiar with theatre practice they should employ a theatre consultant. (The Society of Theatre Consultants will give details of the qualifications and experience of each of its members.)

In the early stages there is temptation to be dangerously optimistic and expert advice is needed if estimates are to be reliably based on actual requirements. The authorizing body must know exactly what is included in estimates of cost and what is not. Any items not included (possibly because there are alternatives requiring policy decisions) should be stated. The fees of architect, quantity surveyor, consultants, etc., must be estimated and there should be some forecast of probable increases in costs, related to a possible building programme. In other words, there must be a realistic attempt to give the probable total of the final bill to be paid, not merely the cost of the building alone. It is grossly misleading if the preliminary estimates suggest, as some do, that the cost of the building is likely to be, perhaps £130,000 but on reading the small print, so to say, one finds that there has not been any provision for such essentials as stage lighting, sound equipment, carpets, curtains, seating, furniture, bar fittings, workshops, external site work and professional fees. The misleading £130,000 is the figure likely to be publicized: recriminations are bound to follow. The authorizing body must beware of such attempts to make the project attractive by playing down supplementary costs that cannot be avoided. If they are misled and begin to get tough when actual costs are soaring above initial estimates, the cuts they insist on will probably mean loss of important accommodation and equipment. It is better to face the brutal truth of realistic planning at the beginning. Any cutting down should be discussed and decided before construction begins.

The architect must be supplied with full details of what is wanted and given some general guidance as to the kind of cost limit that may have to be the basis for his final planning, if it is possible to do so. Any limit suggested must have some sensible relevance to what is being asked for. For example, it would be absurd to propose the current equivalent of a cost based on the Leicester Phoenix (£29,180 in 1963) and to demand something like Nottingham Playhouse (£330,000, also in 1963). Even with the fullest information the architect will have a lot of difficult calculations to make and may have to destroy many initial plans before he can present his proposals with an estimate that is reliably near to any suggested limit.

It is a sound plan for potential members of a board of management to form an *ad hoc* committee in the initial stages (see page 95). One of their most important functions (apt to be overlooked) will be to take account of probable running costs (see page 98), which will be directly influenced by the type of theatre chosen.

Feasibility Study

Before planning for a definite project is authorized and a final brief prepared, provisional design or designs should be produced by an architect, preferably with the co-operation of a theatre consultant unless the architect has the required knowledge of theatre practice. It is not necessary at this stage for an actual site to be chosen: it may, in fact, be an advantage to leave the feasibility study to establish what type and size of site is most likely to be suitable. What must first be decided is the type of theatre that would best suit its purpose. There is bound to be some conflict of opinion about possible alternatives but there must be a decision, preferably unanimous, before the architect is instructed to begin work. For the purpose of his study it would be sufficient to decide:

(*a*) For what purposes the theatre is likely to be used.

(*b*) What form of theatre it is thought would best suit those purposes.

(*c*) The maximum seating capacity likely to be needed.

(*d*) The extent to which, if at all, it should be possible to reduce capacity when a limited audience is expected.

The initial concern should be solely with auditorium and stage. Detailed consideration of ancillary accommodation and equipment is not necessary until after the form and size of theatre have been agreed.

The fees payable for the preliminary study should be negotiated on the understanding that they would be treated as part payment of the standard fees payable if and when the project is definitely commissioned.

It is not sensible to ask the architect to give a serious estimate of the cost at this stage. Until the project is approved and complete sketch plans have been prepared he could only offer an inspired guess at what the final cost could be.

6
A Theoretical Project

It may be useful at this stage to attempt a practical exercise in the preliminary planning of the kind of community theatre that has been discussed. The assumptions that have been made are summarized in the statement supplied to the architect, Robert Adams, who is collaborating in this study:

1. The theatre will be required for varied performances which could include not only plays but also musicals, opera, ballet, revuc and pantomime, which would necessarily be on a modest scale. The performances would be given by visiting professional companies and by local amateur societies. It is not expected that the theatre will be used by a resident repertory company except, perhaps, for occasional limited periods.

2. Concerts are likely to be given by choirs, orchestras, brass bands, pop groups and by individual artists. It is not expected that the theatre would be used by large symphony orchestras.

3. Film shows will be presented and it is possible that both 32 mm and 16 mm projectors would be used.

4. Lectures, meetings and conferences are likely to be housed: projection of films and slides could be involved.

5. Occasional fashion displays and puppet shows are probable.

6. Although a proscenium type of stage appears to be generally favoured there is some interest in the thrust stage and both will be considered. It is probable that most of the visiting theatrical companies and the local amateurs would wish to use scenery. It is essential that whatever type of stage is provided, it must be possible to use scenery effectively. Of those who favour a proscenium stage, a few regard a fly-tower with full flying facilities as necessary. The extent of probable use of a fly-tower may have to be balanced against the extra cost involved and the alternatives must be carefully considered.

7. The total seating capacity should be not less than 650 or more than 700. Either of these capacities would be excessive for some of the proposed activities and it must

be possible to isolate a number of seats, by some simple means, to reduce the effective capacity to about 400.

8. The initial study should be restricted to establishing the stage layout in relation to the auditorium. The ancillary accommodation necessary should be specified in general terms. Bars will be required but it is not proposed to include restaurant service. The possibility of including facilities for exhibitions, meetings, rehearsals, etc., should be considered.

9. The building should be designed for economical construction with standards of finish that are good but not lavish.

10. It is desirable that the preliminary study should establish some approximate estimate of the size of site likely to be required.

7
Alternative Designs for a Community Theatre

by Robert Adams

This design study has been restricted to the stage and its relationship to an auditorium of the seating capacity stipulated.

In the sketch plans which follow current theatre practice is acknowledged and there has been an attempt to find the simplest practical ways of meeting the requirements summarized in Chapter 6.

The proposals must not be judged as a possible standard method of dealing with Community Theatre projects. They must be accepted as illustrating one line of approach, providing subject for discussion so that a final brief may be prepared incorporating any amendments that may be necessary to conform with the policy decisions that are involved.

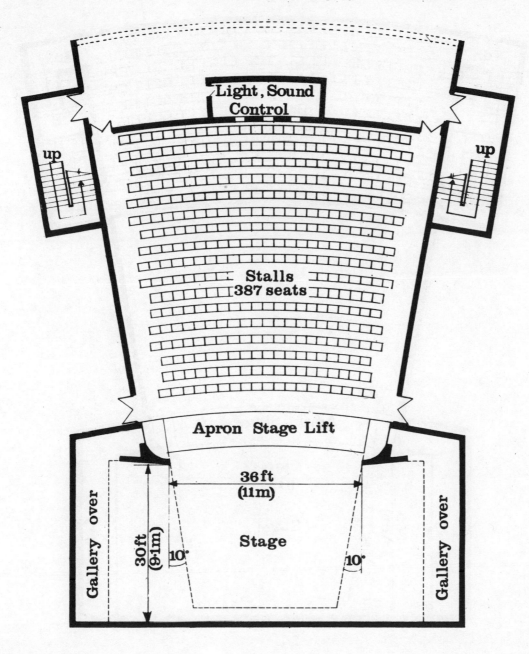

Fig. 16   Alternative 1. Proscenium Stage: Plan showing stage and auditorium with continental seating at Stalls level.

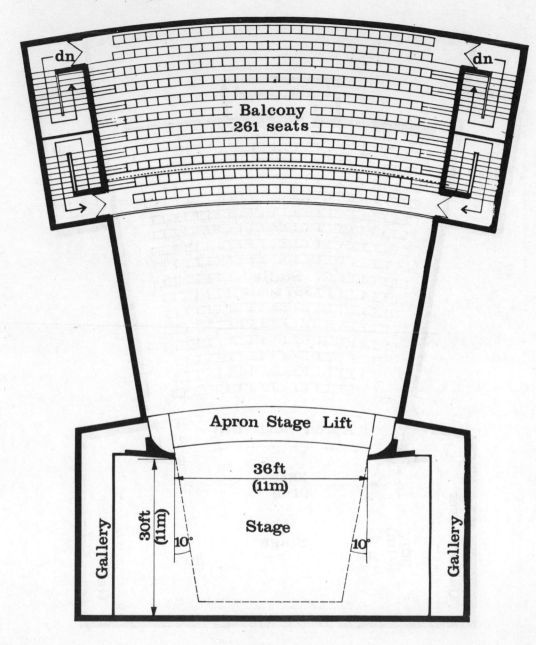

Fig. 17   Alternative 1. Proscenium Stage: Plan showing stage and auditorium with continental seating at Balcony level.

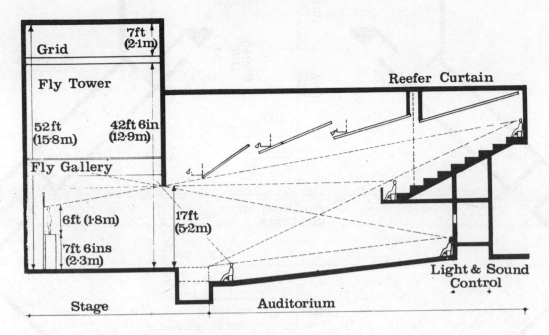

Fig. 18(a)   Alternative 1. Proscenium Stage: Section showing fly-tower and lighting bridges over auditorium.

Fig. 18(b)   Alternative 2. Proscenium Stage: Section without fly-tower showing proposed use of ceiling panels and lighting bridges over auditorium and stage.

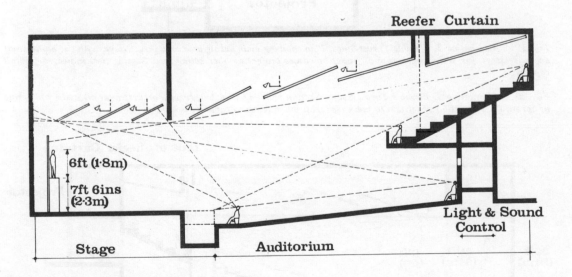

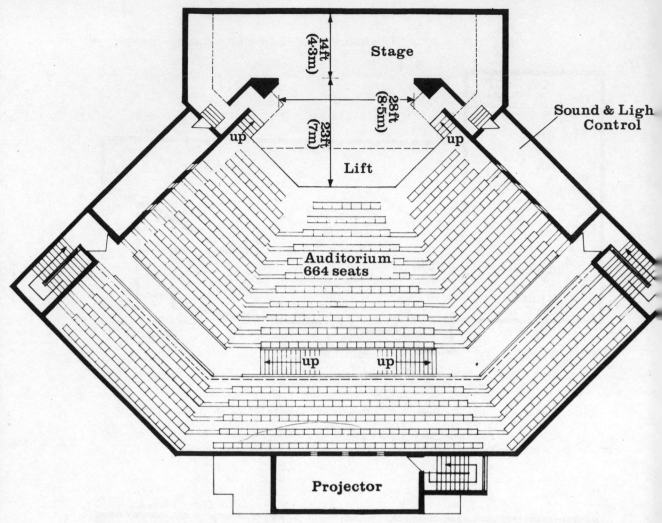

Fig. 19   Alternative 3. Flexible Thrust Stage: Plan showing main acting area on a thrust stage, with the addition of an inner stage for scenic backgrounds. Juliet balconies projecting over acting area. Seating tiers indicated for full capacity.

Fig. 20   Alternative 3. Flexible Thrust Stage: Section showing thrust stage with orchestra pit created by lowering of apron/lift. Indication of curtain to mask rear seats when reduced capacity is needed.

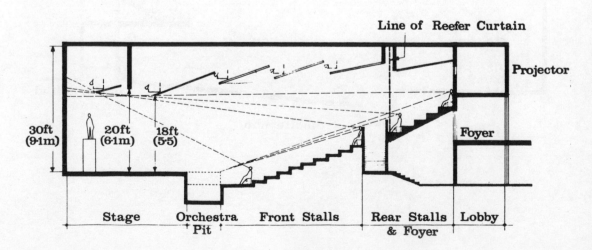

8
General Comment on Architect's Proposals

(a) Proscenium Stage (Alternatives 1 and 2)

The general lay-out conforms with current conventions for this type of theatre and does not suggest any particularly novel features.

Seating Capacity

Continental seating has been adopted. The rows are at 3 ft (0·9 m) centres with 2 ft (0·6 m) arm-to-arm width, providing a good standard of comfort. The total capacity, with an apron lift at stage or at orchestra-pit level is:

Stalls:	387	in 17 rows
Balcony:	261	in 11 rows
Total	648	

If the apron lift were at auditorium level it would be possible to add two rows of seats, 36 in all, increasing the total to 684. By masking all the seats in the balcony beyond the second row the capacity would be reduced to: Stalls 387 plus Balcony 50, a total of 437. The masking would need to span about 60 ft (18·3 m), and could possibly consist of two overlapping trailer curtains, drawn to the sides of the auditorium. This would require a space of about 6 ft (1·8 m) at each side for the curtains when drawn open. This method has not been adopted in the design. It was not convenient to provide the space required and it was considered that a better solution was to use a single vertical reefer curtain which could be drawn up into the roof void. The necessary hauling lines would pass over pulleys at roof-level and would be remotely controlled by push-button operating an electric motor sited in the void (see Fig. 30, page 83). The space above the ceiling as planned would be quite adequate for the purpose. The drop of the curtain below ceiling-level would be about 15 ft (4·6 m).

Sight-lines

It is suggested that the Stalls floor should be ramped to the permitted maximum of

1 in 10, thus making it necessary for the stage to be 3 ft 6 in. (1·1 m) high to provide good sight-lines. If the auditorium were stepped it would be possible to reduce the stage height but the overall height of the building would be increased. The ramp was adopted only to keep down the price: if the extra cost is not a vital concern, the Stalls floor can be stepped when the final plans are produced.

The maximum distance from the side rear seats in the Stalls to the centre-line of the permanent stage is 62 ft (18·9 m) from the second row of the Balcony the distance is 60 ft (18·3 m) and from the rear side seats in the Balcony, 80 ft (24·4 m). These distances are well within the tolerable limits.

Stage

The proscenium opening is 36 ft (11 m) wide and there is 18 ft (5·5 m) wing space at each side. From inside the proscenium wall to the rear wall the depth is 30 ft (9·1 m): in addition there is a permanent apron of 3 ft (0·9 m) the curved front of which follows the line of the curved seating. This apron would be extended, when required, by a lift of 6 ft (1·8 m) making a total stage depth of 39 ft (11·9 m). This lift is restricted to the width of the proscenium opening but there is a permanent apron at each side, approximately 8 ft (2·4 m) x 4 ft (1·2 m), giving a maximum apron width of 45 ft (13·7 m). Access from the stage area to the apron is through side arches with Juliet balconies above.

Stage Lighting Bridges

It will be seen from the section drawing (Fig. 18(a)) that apertures are provided in the ceiling, with lighting bridges above. The siting and the contruction of these bridges will be dealt with in some detail later (see page 89).

Control-room

The stage-lighting control-desk would be placed in a room at the rear of the stalls, underneath the balcony. A position at the rear of the balcony could not be used, of course, as it would be masked when the seating capacity was reduced. This room would also be used for film and slide projection; sound-control could be sited either in this room or on stage and is a matter for discussion. There may be good reasons for selecting an on-stage position.

Fly-tower

If a proscenium stage is chosen it should be assumed that a fly-tower with full flying facilities becomes a normal requirement. Professional touring companies would probably expect to have this provision. Fig. 18(a) includes the fly-tower with a proscenium opening height of 17 ft (5·2 m). The height of 42 ft 6 in (13 m) to the underside of the grid is the minimum to give adequate flying facilities.

It must be assumed that counterweighted lines would be necessary. A fly-gallery at each side is suggested, at about 20 ft (6 m) above stage-level. From these galleries there would be access to the lighting bridges over the auditorium.

Alternative to the Fly-tower

If it is decided that the frequency with which full flying is likely to be needed does not justify the extra cost involved, the alternative shown in Fig. 18(*b*) may be considered.

Fig. 21   Larger-scale section of the proscenium stage without fly-tower (Fig. 18(b))
   A Two-piece safety curtain
   B Main Tabs. (Trailer curtains.)
   C Lighting bridges
   D Intermediate curtains flown on two sets of lines.
   E Rear trailer curtains.

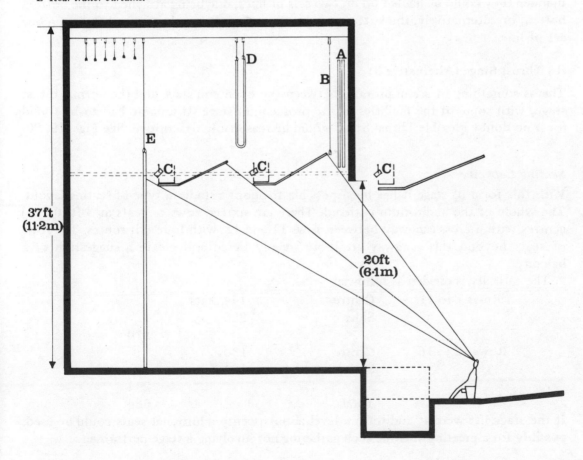

Fig. 21 shows the stage layout in larger scale, which should give a clearer idea of the proposal.

The total height above stage is reduced to 37 ft (11·3 m), a height which is primarily dictated by the height of the auditorium. The volume of the stage tower would be reduced by something like 32,400 cu ft (917 m³). It will be seen that permanent ceiling panels are indicated at the height of the proscenium opening which is now increased to 20 ft (6·1 m). The reasons for having such panels are dealt with in some detail in Chapter 5 (page 37). Borders would be dispensed with and any scenery used would stand freely in front of a neutral curtain surround, or possibly a combination of curtains and cyclorama. As this is a departure from general practice the proposal must be discussed with the people likely to be concerned.

The two ceiling panels cover a stage depth of about 20 ft (6·1 m)and for most drama productions that depth of acting area would be generous. The rear 10 ft (3 m) would be used mainly for background scenery and it would be possible to install a few sets of lines. Although it would not be possible for back-cloths to be flown in the normal manner they could be hauled up on two sets of lines, one being attached to the bottom batten; or, alternatively, the latter could be clipped to the top batten and flown on one set of lines.

(b) Thrust Stage (Alternative 3)

This is something of a compromise between the open end stage and the normal thrust stage, with some of the facilities of the proscenium stage. If a name had to be found for it no doubt Flexible Thrust Stage would be reasonably descriptive. See Figs. 19, 20.

Seating Capacity

With this form of stage it has been possible to adopt a stadium type of seating layout. The whole of the auditorium is tiered. There are sixteen rows of seats at 3 ft (0·9 m) centres with a cross-gangway between rows 11 and 12, with four exit routes. The rows of seats beyond this gangway are more steeply tiered and create a suggestion of a balcony.

The capacity is divided as follows:

Rows 1 to 11	Centre	144 seats	
	Sides	226	
			370
Rows 12 to 16	Centre	130	
	Sides	164	
			294
	Total		664

If the stage lift were at auditorium level about twenty additional seats could be used, possibly for a meeting or some such gathering not involving a stage performance.

To reduce the seating capacity the rear blocks of seats would be masked by vertical reefer curtains as suggested for alternatives 1 and 2. In this case the total length of curtain track would be about 113 ft (34·4 m) and trailer curtains would not be a satisfactory substitute. Push-button operation of a single motor in the roof void would also apply to this installation.

It would thus be possible to reduce the maximum capacity of 664 to 370 when required.

Sight-lines

Because the seating is spread over a much wider area it is unnecessary to have an actual balcony. As the whole of the auditorium is tiered the stage height has been reduced to 3 ft (0·9 m) the tiers below the cross-gangway have 12 in (0·3 m) risers: above the gangway the risers are 18 in (0·45 m). The maximum distance from the end rear seats to the centre of the stage front is 55 ft (16·8 m) and is only about 75 ft (22·9 m) to the rear of the acting area. The sight-lines would be excellent from every seat in the house.

Stage

It must be accepted that this is essentially an open stage. The acting area is a peninsula with a maximum width of 45 ft (13·7 m) and a depth of 23 ft (7 m), which is reduced to 15 ft (4·6 m) if the lift is lowered to create an orchestra pit. There is, however, an inner stage of 14 ft (4·3 m) depth with an opening of 28 ft (8·5 m). The total stage depth is therefore 37 ft (11·3 m). These measurements are rather arbitrary and could be varied if thought necessary.

The space behind the back-stage proscenium is intended to be used primarily for background scenery. It should not be regarded as an extension of the acting area except, perhaps, for spectacular shows with large casts when the extra space would be useful for crowd scenes. For musical shows, with the orchestra pit in use, the main acting area of 15 ft (4·6 m) depth would certainly have to be augmented for chorus work, when the principals would occupy the forward acting area.

There is access from the inner stage to the acting area at each side with Juliet balconies above: these balconies would extend over the stage about 4 ft (1·2 m) providing very useful additional acting levels. There is wing space of 19 ft (5·8 m) at each side of the inner stage, which is quite liberal.

Height above Stage

The total height above the inner stage is 30 ft (9 m) determined by the height of the building. Over the open thrust stage the height is determined by the suspended ceiling panels and varies from 18 ft (5·5 m) to 24 ft (7·3 m). Over the inner stage there is a distance of 6 ft (1·8 m) from the single ceiling panel to the rear wall and in this space there would be a few sets of suspension lines, mainly for curtain track, cinema screen, etc. As there is only 10 ft (3 m) from the top of the opening to the roof beams it is obvious that flying facilities would be minimal and if conventional backcloths were used they would have to be partially rolled before being flown out of sight. It would be an advantage to have a fly gallery at each side, with access to the lighting bridges over stage and auditorium.

Stage-lighting Bridges

Three of the bridges over the auditorium (for what we may call front-of-house lights) would follow the line of the seating to provide the required angular lighting. The one bridge near to the inner stage proscenium and the one inside would be restricted to the width of the opening. In addition there would be lighting slots at each side of the auditorium, with rear access to the lanterns.

Control-room

As the rear of the auditorium would be masked at times the control-room has been sited at the side of the auditorium on stage left. Although the view of the stage from such a position is restricted by comparison with a central rear position, it has been found in practice that a side position is quite effective. For a Community Theatre the direct access from back-stage to the control-room can be an advantage: when stage staff is limited and, of necessity, versatile there is much to be said in favour of having the control staff close at hand. The side position would not prevent easy communication between director and lighting controller during lighting rehearsals. It could, perhaps, be of advantage to the production if the director were to be thus attracted to the side seats. Too often, thrust-stage productions betray the assumption of a central focal point. The projection of films and slides must, of course, be central and a projection room has therefore been placed at the rear of the auditorium. This prevents the use of the masking curtains when the place is used as a cinema but actors on the screen are not disconcerted if they are confronted by empty seats. Their performances will be just as good—or as bad—with or without an audience. For intimate lectures, suitable projectors could be operated from the cross-gangway if the required socket outlets were conveniently sited.

9
Assessment of Alternatives

(1) Proscenium Stage with Fly-tower

This is the form of theatre most widely used by professional companies: few amateurs have the use of a fly-tower, with the exception of those who produce their shows in professional theatres. If the theatre is to be used extensively by touring professional companies the fly-tower should be regarded as a necessity. For all the other probable uses listed the fly-tower could be a disadvantage. The lofty space above stage will be occupied mainly by scenery, curtains and borders, all of which absorb sound. This means that a high standard of voice projection is needed, a standard too rarely achieved by amateurs or by far too many professionals: the latter are so afraid of being "ham" that realistic dialogue often fails to reach the back rows as intelligible speech.

The height and the volume of the stage tower must inevitably push up the cost of the actual building and it is also necessary to equip the grid with a full complement of suspension gear.

(2) Proscenium Stage without Fly-tower

Compared with the stages on which most amateur dramatic societies have to work this would have considerable merit but it would involve a different approach in the design of scenery. This problem was dealt with in some detail in Chapter 4 (page 38). Conventional borders would not be used: scenic flats of any height between 10 ft (3 m) and 18 ft (5·5 m) standing freely in front of neutral draperies would be effective. Cut-out ground-rows in front of a sky-cloth or cyclorama could be used instead of backcloths; this is a technique already familiar to both professional and amateur companies. Professional companies visiting the theatre would be informed in advance of the lack of fly-tower and should be supplied with a plan and section of the stage, when they should have little difficulty in adapting the settings.

For all purposes the acoustics would be improved by the reflection of sound from the ceiling panels. The height and volume of the stage tower would be appreciably reduced and the amount of suspension gear would be limited to about ten sets of lines. The lighting bridges over the stage would be additional but would simplify adjustment and maintenance of the lighting equipment.

(3) Flexible Thrust Stage

This represents greater deviations from established practice and will attract more criticism, particularly from those who are accustomed to and (quite understandably) have a preference for the proscenium stage. For those able and willing to adapt their productions to the open-stage techniques there would not be any serious problems. To assist others to appreciate the possibilities for the varied uses of the stage, the plans and sketches reproduced in Figs. 22-7 should be useful.

The overall height of the building is less than in alternatives 1 and 2 but the plan area occupied would be greater. From the most extreme side seats the view of a cinema screen placed near to the proscenium arch of the inner stage would be rather less favourable than from the worst seats in the proscenium theatre. In alternative 3 the most distant members of the audience would be nearer to the actors than in either of the other alternatives. In alternatives 1 and 2 the acting would have a frontal focus (Stephen Joseph's "linear projection"): in alternative 3 the projection should be inward (Stephen's "organic"). In either case, audiences would be surprised if the differences were to be explained to them. It is only the actors and directors who need to appreciate those differences.

The acoustics of 2 and 3 would be better than alternative 1 and it is probable that 2 would be better than 3 because of the differences of the actors' projection referred to. Competent actors and directors should, however, be able to adjust to the differences, whatever form is chosen.

The final choice of form to be adopted will, no doubt, be determined by the opinions and prejudices of the most influential members of the body whose job it is to make the decision. The choice should be dictated by comparative suitability for the probable uses of the theatre. If it is intended that the main use should be the presentation of stage shows, with a predominance of touring professional companies, it would be logical to choose the proscenium stage complete with fly-tower. If most of the shows are likely to be presented by local amateur companies there is much to be said in favour of the other two alternatives.

If the presentation of film shows is likely to be a frequent activity, the proscenium theatre, with or without fly-tower would be preferable: the fly-tower would be useful as the screen could be flown instead of being rolled.

If the various activities apart from stage shows are of greatest importance the flexible thrust stage could be most suitable. The partial encirclement of the platform by the audience has distinct advantages for concerts, whether orchestral, choral or by individual performers: it would also be very good for lectures and meetings.

The thrust stage form is likely to provoke the greatest interest, both pro and anti. Every effort should be made to get a decision that is unanimous and one that is arrived at on practical grounds rather than on any high-falutin theories. Whatever the decision it is hoped that it will generate collective enthusiasm.

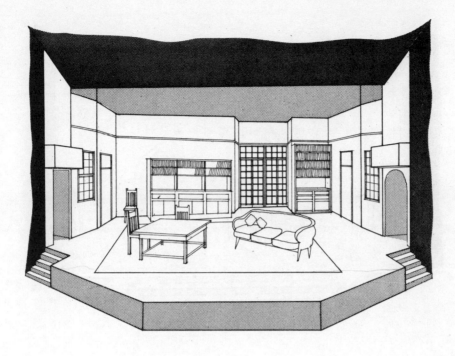

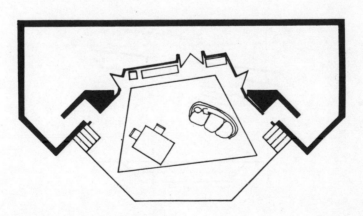

Fig. 22 Flexible Thrust Stage with a conventional-type interior setting. Full stage in use including apron/lift section. Maximum acting depth provided: 23 ft (7 m).

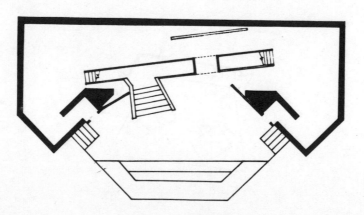

Fig. 23   Flexible Thrust Stage with setting for a classical production, having various acting levels. Cyclorama background. Apron/lift lowered to create step up from auditorium floor. Maximum acting depth provided: 22 ft (6.7 m)

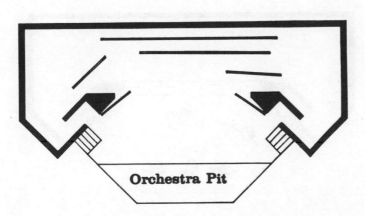

Fig. 24 Flexible Thrust Stage with setting for a musical show. Cyclorama background. Apron/lift lowered to create orchestra pit. Maximum acting depth provided: 18 ft (5·5 m), but this could be increased by omitting one of the scenic ground-rows.

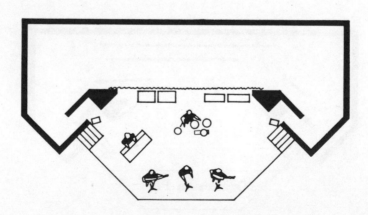

Fig. 25   *Flexible Thrust Stage: Pop group using the full thrust stage, with curtain background.*

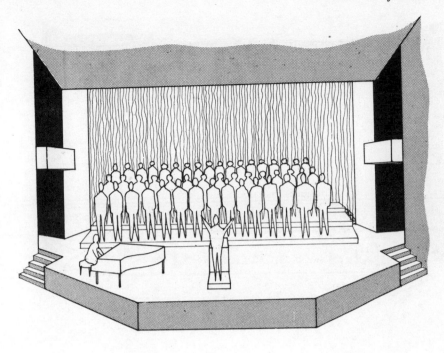

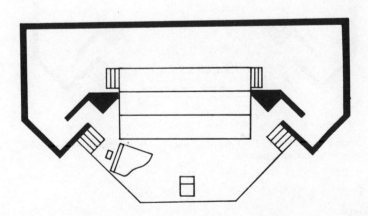

Fig. 26   Flexible Thrust Stage: Area of 22 ft (6·7 m) by 12 ft (3·7 m) occupied by rostrums for choir. Total depth of thrust stage in use.

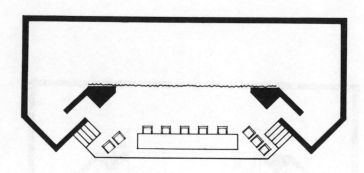

Fig. 27   Flexible Thrust Stage: 12 ft (3·7 m) depth of stage in use as a platform for meetings. Apron/Lift lowered to auditorium level, increasing seating capacity.

Comparative Costs

Complete drawings and quantity lists would be required before it was possible to offer any reliable estimate of the respective costs of the alternative schemes. It would be rash to make any attempt to do so as the prices of materials and the labour costs are, at the time of writing, soaring to unpredictable heights.

Ignoring the cost of land and any exterior amenities, one assumes that the building to house the proscenium stage and fly-tower would be the most expensive. The cost difference between alternatives 2 and 3 is likely to be fairly marginal. The building for alternative 2 has a greater overall height than 3 but the latter requires a greater plan area. The only differences in the ancillary accommodation required would be those caused by the variation of layout.

Area of Site

For either of the proscenium stage theatres the minimum size of site required would be somewhere about 140 ft (42·7 m) by 110 ft (33·5 m); the thrust stage building would need an area of about 160 ft (48·8 m) by 120 ft (36·6 m). These measurements are offered very tentatively as they could be increased by the nature and extent of the ancillary accommodation that may be considered necessary: also they do not include any space required for anything outside the actual building. Choice of site must be affected by its relationship to public and private transport and the need to provide adequate parking space if it does not already exist. The possibility of attracting the maximum number of passing pedestrians must also be borne in mind when the site is being considered.

10
Ancillary Accommodation

The alternative plans that have been examined must be accepted as indicating a line of approach, as methods of dealing with the problems involved. Different and possibly better ways of dealing with the same problems would, no doubt, result from the problems being tackled by people with different ideas.

When a choice of the form of theatre has been made authority should be given for the preparation of sketch plans of the whole building. The front of house and the back-stage accommodation needed will be similar, whatever the form, but the planning will obviously be affected by the stage and auditorium layout. The requirements may involve policy decisions which should be made before the actual planning begins. The probable needs are here examined in general terms only: the allocation of the space available to meet those needs will be related by the architect to his overall design.

Front of House

Main Entrance

It is important that the exterior of the building should be self-explanatory. It must proclaim the fact that it is a theatre and there should not be any doubt about which is the way in. Experience has prompted this apparent emphasis of the obvious. The main entrance should be magnetic in its offer of a warm and friendly welcome. There is a lot of good sense in the provision of the traditional brightly lit canopy over the main doors. Light has a compelling attraction for people as well as for moths. Arriving audiences welcome a reasonably large area of shelter at the spot where they are decanted from their vehicles (public or private) or, if they are pedestrians, where they will pause with welcome relief to lower their umbrellas, recover breath and assume a poise appropriate to the occasion. A generously canopied area outside can also reduce the extent of crowded confusion inside before and after the show.

The entrance should not lead directly from the pavement outside into the foyer. There should be a lobby in which circulation can be diverted. This minimizes congestion and helps to divert those blasts of cold air that chill customers waiting for their less punctual friends.

Foyer

This should be as spacious as the limitations of site and cash available will permit. There must be very clear signs indicating which way the customers must go for what purpose. Circulation must be channelled to avoid congestion during the peak periods when the maximum number of people are assembling or dispersing. There should be an area, preferably raised slightly, where the House Manager may stand to see and be seen by the arriving audience. This position should be near to the box office. The lighting of the foyer should be bright and of a grateful tint: fluorescent tubes are not a good idea for this purpose. Fluorescent lighting, even at its best, creates a hard, cold effect that does not help a woman to achieve maximum glamour at a time when she is likely to be anxious to do so. Even the male likes to look his best when in festive mood and he will be annoyed if his mauve shirt and lavishly figured tie have distorted colours and his complexion has something less than its normal evidence of virility. Lighting throughout the theatre, or any other place of entertainment, should be for communal pleasure, not for utility.

Box Office

It is an old custom, one that cannot be justified, to provide the box-office staff, who are among the most important servants of the theatre, with the least possible space in which to operate. Elizabeth Sweeting emphasizes the qualities needed by these people and the facilities they require in her book *Theatre Administration*, which should be studied. One cannot do better than quote such an authority on the subject of planning the box office:

"Considering the importance of the box office in the hierarchy of theatre staff, the physical conditions in which they work are rarely easy. All too often, even in new buildings, it is assumed that they need only a cubby-hole to work in. In fact, to store adequately their plans, stationery, brochures of the theatre's programmes—sometimes even programmes—they need a lot of storage space. They need on their actual counters a large area for the theatre plans, especially when booking for several plays at a time is in progress. The ease of access to the books of tickets should be made as efficient as possible to reduce the risk of giving tickets from the wrong one, which is all too easy. There should be space for one member of staff to deal with postal booking while another deals personally with customers at the window. Telephones should be easy to reach, so that the plans may be consulted and details written for a telephone booking. Tickets, plans and telephone should all be correctly placed so that one person may deal with all three without moving. Most of the staff's day is spent sitting in one chair at the window, so the chair and the height of the counter must be comfortably planned.

"There are some arguments in favour of an open box office, but strong counter-arguments in favour of making it difficult, if not impossible, for those booking tickets to read the names on the plan or to argue about apparently vacant spaces which may be reserved for a special reason. A more homely argument is for the protection of the staff from the coughs and sneezes and tobacco smoke with which they are constantly assailed."

To her reservations about the open box office idea may be added the risk of making it easy for our modern bandits to grab the takings and make a quick getaway.

The box office should be sited conveniently for the booking of seats when the theatre is not open. It should be near to the main entrance and it must be possible for customers to collect tickets for the current performance without obstructing the entry of those who are arriving for the performance or others who may wish to book for future performances.

Cloak-rooms

In planning for the deposit and collection of hats, coats and other personal impedimenta, it must be remembered that although the deposit may be reasonably leisurely, the collection is a concentrated operation likely to cause congestion and irritation, particularly when people have last buses and trains to catch. In many theatres, because delays in collection are inevitable, there is a prevalent practice of ignoring the cloak-room, coats being dumped underneath the seats in the theatre, where they are liable to get trampled on by the people whose passage along the rows they are obstructing.

A long counter, sited away from the main stream of the departing audience, should make it possible for several attendants to be operating at the same time, spurred on to enthusiastic activity by the constant clatter of coins on the conspicuous saucers. Alternatively, it is now possible to provide self-service: the customer is able to padlock his coat to a specially designed rack and provided he does not lose his key during the show he is able to release his coat without assistance and with the minimum delay. These racks are rather costly and may not be very popular with those members of the staff who are deprived of their "perks."

Toilets

These should be adequate in number for the maximum audience likely to be present. They should be strategically placed for use before the auditorium is entered, possibly at the last minute, and during intervals when there will be maximum use. If at all frequently there are likely to be audiences that are exclusively or mainly juvenile some special consideration should be given to the fact that most of them will lack the height of adults.

Bars

The sale of drinks, snacks, ice cream, chocolates and cigarettes is a necessary activity which, given competent management, can be very profitable. Although the sales of tea, coffee, etc., should be separate from the alcoholic trade it is an advantage if both bars are reasonably near to each other as members of the same party may have different requirements.

The counters of the bars should be as long as possible, with easy circulation to cope with a maximum demand likely to be concentrated in intervals of fifteen minutes each. Unless people can be served quickly, and when served are able to circulate reasonably freely, sales are likely to be lost. Seats, if any, should give maximum service in minimum space: those low and deeply luxuriously upholstered chairs, however welcome they may be for solitary snoozing, are not the sort of furnishing required in theatre bars. A few comfortably padded benches would possibly be adequate, since they would be required for short-term occupation only. Kitchen facilities, whether for snacks or more ambitious feeding, require careful planning: the advice of specialist suppliers will be needed.

Ability to replenish the bars and remove the empties must be carefully studied: the humping of heavy cases over long distances must be avoided.

Offices

The House Manager requires a comfortable office as he is likely to spend long hours on the job. His secretary should be in an adjacent office, and both should be near to the Box Office as there are likely to be frequent consultations. Also, the manager has to be an effective public relations officer in a Community Theatre and should be accessible to the customers. Other FOH administrative offices, if any, could be sited more remotely.

Storage, etc.

There must be adequate space for the storage of stationery, programmes, publicity materials, etc. The cleaners require conveniently sited space for the tools and materials for the job. They and the attendants who sell programmes, usher people to their seats and do other odd jobs should be given some place where they may change their clothing.

Small Hall for Varied Use

There should be some accommodation for meetings, intimate lectures and other purposes. There is much to be said in favour of having a club whose members are closely identified with the theatre. It could have a variety of interests probably involving appointment of committees who would need a place where they could meet. The local amateurs would probably welcome a room in which they could rehearse and possibly present experimental productions to limited audiences. A size of, say, 40 ft

(12·2 m) square could be suitable, especially if it could be partitioned to form two rooms when necessary. If possible, there should be a separate entrance to allow use of the room without the people concerned having to pass through the theatre foyer. This is a matter that should be discussed with the people who are likely to be concerned, so that the architect can be given a clear lead. A room of this type could be a source of useful revenue.

Back-stage and Associated Accommodation

Stage Door

There should be a doorkeeper's office near to the back-stage entrance. Even though a full-time stage-doorkeeper may not be necessary there will be many occasions when one would be required to keep out undesirable gate-crashers. There should be a clear view of the stage door from the office, if the overall planning permits.

Dressing-rooms

These should be sited as conveniently as possible to the stage. Opinions differ about the number of people who should be accommodated in each room. In a Community Theatre it is unlikely that "star" dressing-rooms will be demanded but when professional companies are visiting it is quite possible that the leading players will expect some special consideration.

It would be sensible to provide six rooms of modest size, say 12 ft (3·7 m) square plus two large rooms likely to be used by members of the chorus or supers required for crowd scenes. Each room should have its wash-basin with hot and cold water. Toilets and showers should be convenient to all rooms. As it is still customary to segregate the sexes it should be possible to vary the grouping of the dressing-rooms and toilets as the respective numbers of males and females are likely to differ from show to show.

Make-up tables would normally be of a bench type, fixed to the wall, with a mirror at each make-up position. The seated actor should be near to the mirror: a bench depth of about 18 in. (0·5 m) would be satisfactory. The mirror should not be surrounded by naked lamps although this is an all too common practice—the result being that on entering a dressing-room one is blinded by a blaze of light, most of which is wasted. The lamps should be in reflectors, the angle of which should be adjustable so that whether the actor is seated or standing the light can be directed to both sides of the face. Two 150-watt lamps in reflectors would be far more effective and far less expensive in current consumption than a dozen 60-watt naked lamps jutting out at top and sides.

Fluorescent lighting must not be used in dressing-rooms: the colour value of the fluorescent light differs from that of the tungsten light by which the stage is certain to be lit.

The dressing-rooms must have racks for the storage of costumes on hangers. Each actor may have several changes of costume. The racks should be sited to cause the minimum amount of obstruction.

Although the major use of the dressing-rooms will be during hours of darkness there will be many times when daylight need not be excluded. It is not a good idea to create windowless cells, which can be very depressing and claustrophobic; and curtains could give a nice touch of brightness to the place.

Wardrobe

Although it is unlikely that any of the companies using the theatre will design and make costumes on the premises a wardrobe mistress is likely to be needed to receive and distribute the costumes, execute running repairs and perhaps do a little washing and ironing. Costumes are likely to be delivered in bulky skips, for the handling and storage of which there must be adequate space. The washing and ironing facilities should not be for the exclusive use of the wardrobe mistress: the ladies of touring companies should be discouraged from washing their smalls in the dressing-rooms.

In the wardrobe-room there should be a large table, a sewing-machine and a robing-mirror. The lighting—tungsten of course—should be generous.

Canteen

Performers and stage staff often have to be in the theatre for long periods during which they need refreshment: frequent cups of tea are likely to be minimum requirements. If the kitchen serving the FOH bar can also conveniently serve the stage personnel so much the better. It is useful if there can be a separate room in which the tea and coffee can be made and/or served to avoid having the dressing-rooms littered with cups and saucers or (more probably) with just cups or mugs.

Stage Accommodation

Scene-dock

This should be an area adjoining the actual stage and separate from the wing space. It is the area required for unloading and stacking scenery and properties before being transferred to the stage wings or acting area. The floor-level should be that of the stage and should be raised above the outside ground-level to minimize the labour needed to load and unload vehicles. It should be possible for these vehicles to reverse close to the loading-door: in planning this external space it must be borne in mind that the vehicles in question are likely to be large and high vans. The scene-dock doors should be wide and high to accommodate the awkward shapes and sizes of the articles handled.

Storage of Stock Scenery, etc.

During the years the theatre will accumulate stocks of miscellaneous scenery flats, rostrums, properties, furniture and various odds and ends. If provision is to be made for performances by choirs and orchestras, the number of rostrums to be stored is likely to be considerable (see page 85): chairs are also likely to be stored. Space must be available for the purpose, with reasonable access to the stage and without causing congestion. This space will be scrutinized critically by the local fire officer.

Scenic Workshops

If there is not to be a resident professional company it will probably be thought unnecessary to provide a carpenters' shop or facilities for painting cloths and flats. This is, however, a matter that should be carefully considered in the early planning period. It is possible that space and equipment may be needed if the theatre is likely to have an associated amateur organization responsible for presenting regular productions, in which case they will certainly need some workshop accommodation. A carpenters' workshop needs space for a wood-working bench, canvasing bench, timber-racks, tools and possibly a few machines. There must also be space for assembly and enough height to allow easy handling of flats, which could be 18 ft (5·5 m). The paint room may have to accommodate cloths on battens which could be about 40 ft (12 m) long. There must be access between the two workshops and from both to the stage and there must be room for the unloading and storage of long lengths of timber and sheets of 3-ply and hardboard. The architect will certainly need expert advice if the space available is to be planned effectively for its intended use.

Electrician's Store

This would also have to serve as an occasional workshop and a suitable bench should be provided. Stocks of electrical accessories would have to be stored for the whole theatre and shelf space should be liberal. A special storage rack would be needed for large sheets of colour filters, probably 4 ft (1·2 m) by 2 ft (0·6 m) plan size, with a series of shelves to allow the sheets to be stored flat. This store should be reasonably close to the stage.

Stage Manager's Office

This must lead directly to the stage and should be as near as possible to the prompt corner (see below). The most important duties of the stage manager are not performed in the office but there are many times when he needs a desk or table which should be large enough to allow plans to be spread and studied. This office should not be a cramped cubicle: it should be large enough for two persons to work in some comfort, as the stage manager of a visiting company may have to share the office at times. There should be shelves for storage of miscellaneous articles frequently needed by the stage manager.

Prompt Corner

This is the position from which the stage manager controls the entire performance. In the proscenium theatre it has been traditional for the prompt corner to be sited on stage left, near to the edge of the proscenium arch: as a result, stage left has become known as Prompt Side (PS) and stage right is usually referred to as the OP side, i.e. opposite prompt. In practice the prompt corner may be on either side. From the control position the stage manager should be able to see clearly both the acting area and the wing space on his side. It is an advantage if he can also see the entrance used by the actors.

From the prompt corner the stage manager must be able to signal to foyer, bars, lighting control, projection-room, orchestra, fly-galleries and other outstations, perhaps a dozen in all.

The Association of British Theatre Technicians in collaboration with the West End Stage Managerial Association has published an Information Sheet (No. 4) with the title: *Prompt Corner: Layout and Equipment.* Although something less elaborate than the equipment required for a large professional theatre would serve for our Community Theatre, the principles involved are the same. There is need here for expert advice.

Stage Basement

The space below the stage can be useful for a variety of purposes but the fire authorities are not enthusiastic about having such an area which, unless there was great vigilance, could rapidly acquire a clutter of combustible articles. Suitable fire precautions would certainly be demanded. The stage floor above should consist of 1¼ in. (32 mm) hardwood T&G boards which have greater fire-resistance than softwood: if the latter is used the fire authority may insist on a thickness of 2 in. (50 mm) unless it is laid directly on concrete.

If there is an apron lift or there are stage traps the basement is an obvious necessity. There should be access from each side of the stage and the height should not be less than 7 ft (2·1 m).

Traps

The old traditional traps of assorted types are now mainly of historical interest. The slick performers who were wont to display acrobatic expertise in split-second usage of traps are no longer to be seen. There is a new fashion in traps which, like most new fashions, is an old one that has been refurbished. This requires the whole or part of the acting area to be in modular sections which may be removed selectively to provide any number of cute subterranean entrances and exits, which can be ever so much fun for all concerned.

The Grand Theatre, Leeds, must be one of the few remaining old theatres in England which had an acting area consisting of lifts running from side to side (common enough in the European Opera houses) but as they had not been in use for years they are now covered by an unbroken stage floor. Lifts of this type could quickly transform a Community Theatre stage into a tiered Concert Hall platform but the cost could hardly be justified by need: portable rostrums would be very much cheaper and rather more versatile.

A grave trap, not less than 6 x 3 ft (1·8 x 0·9 m), could often be useful. The top must be carefully made to fit flush and it should not squeak in protest when it is walked on.

Orchestra Pit

The lift, which can create either an apron stage or an orchestra pit, has become a fairly standard requirement. In planning the pit about 10 sq ft (0·93 m²) should be allowed for each player, plus 50 sq ft (4·65 m²) for the piano and about the same for the drummer's bulky collection of instruments. The lifts indicated in the two alternative projects dealt with in Chapter 8 would not be adequate for such large orchestras as are normally needed in major productions of opera and ballet but should suffice for performances likely to be staged in the type of theatre proposed. The number of players likely to need accommodation in the pit should be discussed before the lift/apron/pit is planned.

The floor-depth of the pit below stage-level would be adjustable, but the limit must not be less than 6 ft (1·8 m): only the conductor need be partially visible to actors and audience.

The lights on the music-stands should be shaded to limit the spill of light from the pit and it is useful in a stage black-out if the orchestra lights can be dimmed by the conductor.

Although the musicians should have access to the pit from the stage basement the conductor should be able to make his entrance via the front gangway to provoke the applause he expects when he appears.

Band-room

The musicians require a room in which to deposit outer clothes, etc., a room to which they may also retire for cups of tea or more stimulating refreshment when they are not needed in the pit. It may not be justifiable to provide a room for their exclusive use but one should be conveniently available when the need arises.

Electrical Mains

There must be early consultation with the Electricity Board and arrangements made to ensure that the total supply of current to the theatre will not only be adequate for initial needs but will provide a margin for possible future additions. Protected accommodation for the switchgear should be sited as near as possible to the external mains to avoid the cost of long runs of heavy cables.

Battery-room

Special housing must be provided for the storage batteries needed for the emergency lighting. This room must have good independent ventilation direct to the open air to prevent accumulation of the noxious fumes that may be generated. Strict safety precautions are necessary.

Access Between Stage and FOH

It must be possible for those people whose duties involve movement between stage area and the rest of the building to be able to avoid passing through the auditorium. There should, however, be some access, preferably at the stage end, for those occasions when it is needed, as in the case of the orchestra conductor already mentioned. In addition, it is useful to have steps leading from auditorium to stage: for some of the probable uses of a Community Theatre it would be a disadvantage not to have these steps.

Control-room

As the control of stage lighting should be in a position that gives the operator a clear view of the stage the room must be planned in relation to the general layout of the front-of-house accommodation but it may be more logical to discuss it with the general stage requirements.

A position at the rear of the auditorium is best but if a rear position is not convenient an acceptable alternative could be at one side of the auditorium (see Chapter 8, page 56). The control-room should have a window through which the operator has a clear view of the stage whether he is seated or standing. The window should slide open to allow two-way speaking (or shouting) between auditorium and control-room during rehearsals. The distance between the operator and the window should be dictated only by the size of the control-panel: he should be as near as possible, not pushed back by inserted desk space. There should be localized down-lighting to avoid spill into the auditorium and to prevent the window becoming a mirror. The general lighting of the room must have conveniently placed switches.

As it is necessary to work to both aural and visual cues, the sounds coming from the stage must be relayed to the control position and the operator must be able to control volume. There must also be talk-back communication with the stage manager and exchange of signals.

It is quite common practice to site the sound-control in a FOH position but for a theatre with very varied uses it may be thought better to have control on the stage near to the prompt corner. There are valid arguments in favour of either position. If the sound and lighting controls are placed in the same control-room the space allowed should be reasonably generous and if possible the two should be separated by a partition. It must not be assumed that one operator can cope with both controls. This may be possible on some occasions but more frequently each control will require its own operator, as both will have to respond simultaneously to some of the cues.

Projection-room

A separate room should be provided for film projection if possible, and this must be in a central position to avoid distortion of the picture. There are established standards affecting the planning of projection-rooms and there should be consultations with the equipment suppliers and the local authority whose approval is necessary.

There should be suitable space for any projector that may be required to show advertisement slides, quite a profitable activity. It must also be possible to accommodate follow-spots: two should be adequate. If their use (or misuse) is not likely to be frequent it is possible that the lanterns could be hired by the people wishing to have them: socket outlets would be needed in suitable positions. In fixing the sites for follow spots it must be remembered that they should be able to throw their emphatic pools of light on any part of the stage. It might be necessary to spot the face of a performer who is standing on a high rostrum up-stage. The use of follow spots is dealt with later (see page 88).

The planning of the spaces for control and projection will need some expert guidance. Too often the needs are underestimated. The technicians who have to take such important parts in the control of performances often have to work for long periods of stress and tension, and they are entitled to have a modicum of comfort. They should be able to move about freely and the ventilation system should provide them with air that is not more than normally polluted.

11
Equipment of Stage

(i) General

Safety-curtain

The purpose of the safety-curtain is to seal off the stage area from the auditorium so that in the event of a fire on-stage the smoke and fumes may be isolated long enough to enable the audience to leave without panic. When the safety-curtain is down the fire would quickly cause a build-up of pressure which must be released through roof vents in what is known as the lantern light. The vents must fall open when fusible links are subjected to heat and the glass must be thin enough to break quickly. If it were not for the latter requirement glass would not be used at all as any daylight above the stage is definitely not wanted: the glass should be painted black. Above the safety-curtain there must be a drencher system whose main purpose is to prevent buckling of the curtain which should be constructed of steel covered with asbestos cloth. Some authorities will accept a framed asbestos curtain without steel plates. Any safety-curtain must have a gravity descent at the rate of a foot per second and there must be emergency releases, one in the prompt corner and the other external to the stage.

Fig. 28 shows a typical rigid safety-curtain, a type which must be installed if there is sufficient height above stage. If the height is restricted a two-piece or even a three-piece rigid curtain would be acceptable. These are generally similar in construction but the sections must overlap in smoke-proof joints; the lower sections move more quickly and the speed is adjusted so that all sections complete the travel simultaneously. If space is not available for any of the rigid types it would be necessary to have a roller curtain of asbestos cloth made to a standard specification. The diameter of the roller is dictated by the length of span: it is likely to occupy a lot of head-room immediately inside the proscenium opening and therefore to restrict the space available for other equipment. Any type of safety-curtain must overlap the opening by 18 in. (0·46 m) at the top and at each vertical edge.

Although the requirement to install a safety-curtain is to some extent governed by the seating capacity and the plan area of the stage it is a matter to be decided by the local Fire authority: there should be early consultation. It is obviously not practical to demand a safety-curtain for most types of open stage but it is customary for the authority to insist on fire-resistance of materials used for scenery, etc.

Fig. 28   Single-piece framed asbestos-cloth safety-curtain installed in the Thorndike Theatre, Leatherhead.

Suspension Gear

The old traditional method of suspending equipment over the stage was to use sets of three hemp ropes passing over pulleys fixed to the grid, with a triple-head pulley sited above the rail fixed to the front of the fly-gallery, the ropes being tied off to cleats. To make extensive changes of scenery could involve a lot of brawn and skill, and although payment in the old days was at meagre rates the total cost for an ambitious production could be considerable. In any new theatre with a fly-tower the ropes would be replaced by steel cables and the weight of the suspended scenery would be balanced by weights in cradles travelling in vertical guides. Fig. 29 shows the sectional arrangement of a

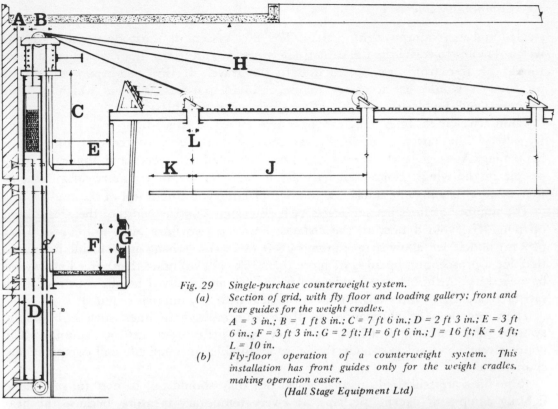

Fig. 29   Single-purchase counterweight system.
   (a)   Section of grid, with fly floor and loading gallery; front and
rear guides for the weight cradles.
A = 3 in.; B = 1 ft 8 in.; C = 7 ft 6 in.; D = 2 ft 3 in.; E = 3 ft
6 in.; F = 3 ft 3 in.; G = 2 ft; H = 6 ft 6 in.; J = 16 ft; K = 4 ft;
L = 10 in.
   (b)   Fly-floor operation of a counterweight system. This
installation has front guides only for the weight cradles,
making operation easier.
            (Hall Stage Equipment Ltd)

single-purchase counterweight system. For this system it must be possible for the weight-cradles to travel the full distance between grid and stage floor, and one side wall should be free from any obstruction to the travel. If this clear space cannot be provided it would be necessary to use a double-purchase system, which is more expensive and doubles the number of weights needed to achieve a balance.

Counterweighted lines may be operated either at stage-floor-level or from the fly-gallery: the latter is preferable as the fly-man has a better view of what is happening. At stage-level the view could be obstructed by scenery and properties or by people in the wings. Horizontal rails should be fitted to the counterweight frame so that scenery flats may be stacked without interfering with the travel of the cradles.

The number of lines per set necessary is determined by the width of the proscenium opening. To avoid deflection the distance between two lines must not exceed 16 ft (4·9 m) and if we allow a maximum of 4 ft (1·2 m) overhang at each side it follows that for a proscenium opening of more than 36 ft (11 m) more than three lines would be necessary. Although it would be difficult for any man to handle four rope lines satisfactorily the counterweight system can deal with any number required.

There are possible alternatives to these counterweighted lines, such as hydraulic systems and electric winches, but they are little used in this country. The counterweight system is usually the most acceptable: it is reliable and comparatively economical.

Rope lines are still used on small stages but they should not be used for suspended lighting equipment except, perhaps, as a very temporary measure, because the heat from the lanterns would cause deterioration of the rope with possible fatal consequences. Wire cables are necessary and if not counterweighted they can be operated by self-sustaining hand winches. A few rope lines could be inserted between counterweighted lines for occasional special use.

It is usual to space sets of lines at 6 in. (150 mm) centres, which allow reasonable choice of suspension positions.

Fly-galleries

When theatre grids were universally fitted with hand-lines fly-galleries were necessary to sustain the ropes tied to the cleats on the front rails. When anything was suspended at full height there could be an awful lot of rope lying around and the galleries tended to be very wide. They had also to be very substantial as they had to take the weight of all the suspended equipment: it is usual to allow for a point load of 300 lb (136 kg) on the grid. The fly-gallery for a counterweight system does not need a depth of more than about 4 ft (1·2 m), but the total projection from the wall would be increased by the depth of the frame carrying the weight cradles, 2 ft 6 in. (0·8 m): allowance for a total projection of 7 ft (2 m) would be sensible.

Although the counterweights would be concentrated on one side of the stage a gallery on the opposite side would be useful and is normally provided. The few rope sets required for occasional use could be used from that side. Both galleries could provide positions for special lighting effects and all lighting equipment suspended over the acting area should be connected to socket outlets on the galleries.

The fly-floors should be high enough to allow scenery flats to be stacked underneath. It is unlikely that many flats would be higher than 18 ft (5·5 m) and it would be reasonable to fix the height of the gallery at 20 ft (6 m) above the stage floor.

The distance between the two fly-galleries should allow for the clearance of the widest cloths likely to be used. There should be clear space for at least 6 ft (1·8 m) on each side of the proscenium opening. Thus if the opening is 36 ft (11 m) wide the distance between the two fly-rails would be not less than 36 ft plus 12 ft = 48 ft (11 m + 3·6 m = 14·6 m) and the width of the fly-tower would be a minimum of 48 ft plus 14 ft = 62 ft (14·6 m + 4·3 m = 18·9 m). If the fly-tower is limited to these measurements the wing space at each side would be less than the desirable minimum of half the width of the proscenium opening and any additional wing space beyond the fly-tower walls should not be less than 20 ft (6·1 m) high. This arrangement would make it necessary to use double-purchase counterweighting (see page 80) and should be avoided if possible. In the case of the project dealt with in Chapters 7 and 8 the galleries should also give access to the lighting bridges over the auditorium and, in the alternatives 2 and 3, over the stage.

Cyclorama

In its original form this completely enclosed the acting area, extending as high as possible, and could eliminate or reduce the need for side wings and borders. A cyclorama must present a plain surface on which light and colour may be projected. Complete enclosure of the acting area is of dubious value: entrances and exits become complicated, or at any rate restricted, and if such a cyclorama cloth is flown there may be obstruction of the grid. A more elaborate form is one in which the cloth enclosing the acting area is drawn along a suspended track and rolls into an end column.

The alternative most frequently adopted for the small stage is to plaster the back wall which is painted off-white or possibly pale blue or it may be stippled: there have been various fashions from time to time but as the colour in the light can be altered to suit the need the off-white treatment is probably the best. The disadvantage of the back-wall cyclorama is that its surface may suffer maltreatment by those scene-shifters who are unable to resist the temptation to stack scenery and props against it: the realism of fleecy clouds in a summer sky is not aided by a chipped surface and the imprints of dirty hands. Nevertheless, the back-wall cyclorama is very useful and on many stages it is kept in decent condition. An alternative is to use a canvas cloth laced to a frame and stretched to give a taut surface or a simple sky-cloth, battened top and bottom, and flown or rolled like any other drop-cloth.

For the Community Theatre the plastering of the rear wall should be a reasonable way of dealing with the cyclorama requirement. The plastering must be expertly done in a continuous operation to avoid imperfections which are certain to be emphasized when the surface is lit from above and below. A smooth matt finish is usual but there have been quite successful experiments with granular finishes, which may give a more dispersive reflection of the light.

Curtains and Curtain Tracks

There are many types of curtain tracks which have been specially designed for stage use. Even on the very small stage it is not a good idea to use the tracks intended for domestic use. Stage tracks have to be free in movement and robust enough to cope with the heavy curtains and with the vigorous operation that is sometimes necessary. The minimum requirements for our type of Community Theatre are likely to be:

(a) *House Tabs.* Known also as Main Tabs or Act Drop, the latter rather dubiously as it originally referred to a painted cloth or curtain which was independent of the House Tabs and was lowered at the end of each act. Any one of these terms may now refer to the curtains immediately behind the proscenium arch to separate the stage from the auditorium. There must be two overlapping curtains no matter whether they are drawn off to the sides or are hauled up into the flys. It must be possible for leading performers to make those appearances, with simulated reluctance, in response to the persistent applause after the final curtain has fallen. Even if there is a fly-tower the curtains should be on a track which enables them to be drawn open, if required. Festoon curtains, at one time very popular but now rarely used, remain fixed at the top as they are pulled upwards and sideways simultaneously to hang in graceful drapes. The House Tabs may be electrically operated, if desired, but the control motor must have infinitely variable speeds for theatrical use: for cinema or other uses selection of a fixed speed is usually satisfactory.

(b) *Traverse Curtains.* These are suspended over the acting area and are usually operated by hand-lines in the wings, or possibly by a hand-winch fixed to the stage floor if the curtains are too large and heavy to be operated smoothly by hand. It is customary to have one set of curtains (often referred to as the No. 1 Trailers) about 6 ft (1·8 m) up-stage, creating a fore-stage on which scenes may be played as the setting behind is changed.

(c) *Rear Trailers.* As the name implies these are suspended at the rear of the acting area. The actual position in which they are used should be variable. If there is a grid with suspension lines it is a simple matter to move the curtains up or down stage. They are operated similarly to the Traverse Curtains.

(d) *Leg Curtains.* These are suspended at the sides of the acting area to act as wings. They may be tied to suspension barrels or to swivel-arms which allow the curtains to be used at whatever angle is suitable, or they could form a continuous run at each side. Alternatively, the leg curtains could be attached to the type of frames normally covered with scenic canvas, in which case there would probably be two frames hinged together forming what is known as a book-wing. If it is intended that scenery of restricted height should stand freely in front of a curtain surround (as was suggested in previous chapters) the curtain lay-out should be carefully planned with this in mind. The curtains cannot be allowed to obstruct windows, doors or other openings in the set. If possible, the curtains should be hauled up to a position a little below the tops of the flats or, if the necessary suspension gear is not available, it may be necessary to use curtains made specially for the job, or normal curtains may be looped up to the required height, being secured with hooks, clips or studs in the appropriate places: as a not very satisfactory substitute, safety-pins may be necessary.

(e) *Reefer Curtains.* This is one of the many nautical terms understandably appropriated by the theatre in its use of ropes. It is used to describe a curtain which is drawn into folds from the bottom upwards by a number of vertical lines at regular intervals, the fabric forming gracefully curved swags or festoons: it is sometimes referred to as a Festoon Curtain. In the schemes dealt with in Chapters 7 to 8 it has been suggested that Reefer Curtains should be used to mask the rear seats to reduce the capacity. Fig. 30 shows the method of suspending these curtains.

Fig. 30   Reefer (Vertical Festoon) Curtain
    A, electric motor unit; B, multi-line clew; C, single cable sheave; D, multi-line head sheave; E, swivel festoon pulley; F, clew guide lines; G, festoon barrel; H, curtain tie tapes; J, clew guide tensiones

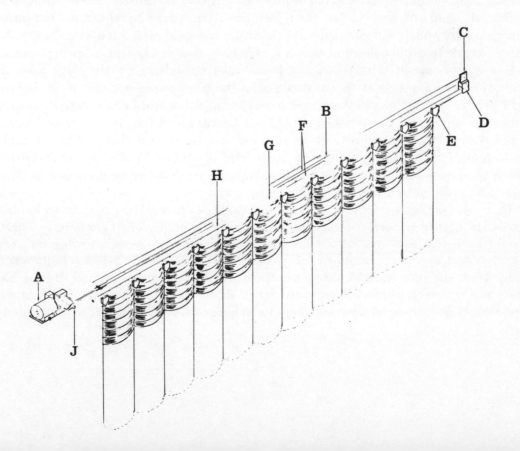

If a theatre is likely to be used for cabaret, revue or concert party shows it is useful to have a festoon curtain of satin or other similar fabric with a sheen. Changes of colour lighting from various angles can create a selection of attractive backgrounds.

(*f*) *Borders.* The use of borders is dealt with in Chapter 4 and the possible use of ceiling panels as an alternative is suggested. If borders are required they should be carefully planned to provide the most effective masking with the minimum of obstruction to the stage lighting. They should intrude into the stage setting as little as possible. If they are needed to be an actual part of the setting they would probably be specially made and painted. Borders used with stage curtains would normally be made of the same material and the same colour. They should have fullness if they are to hang at all gracefully when tied to the suspension barrels. At best, borders can be a necessary evil: at worst they are an evil that is probably not necessary.

Planning the Curtains

This is a job that requires the careful attention of somebody who is familiar with the problems involved. There are many tricky sight-lines to be considered and it is quite possible that two different firms of suppliers would submit two different schemes.

The fabric from which the house tabs are made will almost certainly be chosen by the architect as they create the dominant focal point in the auditorium and must be complementary to the general décor. The colours in the carpets, seats and curtains will determine the effect on the audience as they enter. Extravagant designs for the House Tabs should be considered warily—and usually discarded. These curtains are quite costly and will have to last for a long time. What may be wildly and temptingly contemporary today will probably be frightfully old-fashioned a few years hence. It is also advisable to avoid pale tints, which are likely to show early signs of being soiled.

If a safety-curtain is installed the house tabs must hang on the stage side: this applies also to any pelmet that is used unless the proscenium opening is reduced by a rigid pelmet outside the safety curtain and of a similar fireproof construction. The high unbroken surface of the curtains should not be sacrificed too lightly: they are more impressive without a pelmet. If it is necessary to reduce the effective height a proscenium border could be used as mentioned in Chapter 4. Unless the material of which the house tabs are made is thick and opaque they should be lined and the lining should be easily detached when cleaning is necessary.

There should be a complete set of stage draperies of uniform texture and colour, consisting of the trailers, leg curtains and borders (if used). The Community Theatre should have two sets, one of a colour suitable for general use as a setting for varied purposes and the other should be either black or a deep blue. Cotton velours was for many years the most suitable fabric but there are now available materials of man-made fibres giving greater choice. If only one set of draperies is provided the black or dark blue should be chosen as they are likely to be needed for the drapery surround used as the background for the cut-down scenery flats already referred to several times.

All stage draperies must be fire-resistant and must hang in graceful folds: a fullness of 50 percent must be specified, i.e. a finished curtain, after the fullness has been gathered and sewn to the top webbing, would be two-thirds of the width of the curtain before the fullness is created. In order to keep down a competitive price there is sometimes a temptation to allow only 33⅓ percent fullness which is inadequate: quotations should be carefully scrutinized. The actual yardage of material to be used should be asked for.

Stage Rostrums

In theatrical parlance the plural of rostrum is rostrums: in educational establishments the stage people appear to be intimidated by academic niceties and use rostra.

If the stage is intended to be used at times as a concert platform for choirs and orchestras it should be possible to create tiers deep enough to accommodate musicians, stands and instruments for which a minimum depth of 5 ft (1·5 m) is needed. Choirs could manage quite well with a depth of 3 ft (1 m) and that depth would normally be more suitable for the general use of rostrums in stage settings. The likely extent of the respective uses should be discussed. It may be possible to use a standard module of 3 ft (1 m) perhaps with lengths of 6 ft (2 m) and 9 ft (3 m). Although the resultant arrangement of tiers for orchestras would be more generous in depth than may be necessary, the general usefulness of the rostrums could be increased. There should be some careful planning to ensure maximum flexibility. The risers should not be less than 12 in. (305 mm) and it may be desirable to have more frames of varying heights than tops to fit the frames. The latter should fold when the tops are removed to reduce storage space needed and to improve portability.

If it is intended that a multi-purpose room should be available for experimental productions, the rostrums would be required for the audience seating in which case the height of the risers should be 1 ft 4 in. (406 mm) to allow the acting area to be at floor-level.

The rostrums would also be useful to provide platform accommodation for the VIPs at meetings and conferences: they like to be seen as well as to see clearly.

Although the rostrums could be added at any time they are necessary equipment for a Community Theatre and should be included in the initial specification.

Stage-cloth

For most purposes it is desirable that the stage floor should be covered. In any case it should not be the highly polished floor that is so favoured in school assembly halls. For stage performances the whole of the acting area plus a margin of about 6 ft (2 m) all round, should be covered. The usual stage-cloth is made of strong cotton duck which used to be called sail-cloth but on some stages a thick plain linoleum is used. The latter is less liable to damage by the "running" of scenery flats by energetic stage hands, but the surface can become rather slippery.

Cine Screens

The size and type of screen to be selected from the wide variety available must depend on the purposes for which it is to be used and on the type of projectors to be installed. The advice of the specialist suppliers should be obtained.

Whatever type of screen is installed, together with its ancillary sound equipment, it must be possible for it to be placed in position and removed after use with the minimum of labour and time. The use of the theatre as a cinema will probably be spasmodic but it is almost certain that the change-over must be made quickly.

(ii) Stage Lighting

General Principles

It should be sufficient to deal very broadly with the requirements. There are a number of books which deal comprehensively with the art and technique of stage lighting and if necessary these should be studied by the people most directly concerned with the problems. During the last thirty years or so stage-lighting techniques have altered considerably. This fact was emphasized by Frederick Bentham in an article which appeared in *TABS* in March 1972, when he reminded us that in 1932 the Royal Shakespeare Theatre, Stratford-upon-Avon (then the Shakespeare Memorial Theatre), had a manually operated grand master switchboard with only 56 dimmers, which was rather lavish at that time, whereas in 1972 they installed what Bentham described as "the first completely computer based lighting control in any theatre in Europe. In fact, as far as I know, in the world." This control has 240 dimmers, the actual grouping of which presents no problem as, Bentham adds, "all that can be left to the computer and the instant memory system. Of presets the operator has 250 so to speak and within three minutes by tape cassette Dump store the unlimited credit of a Monte Cristo."

It is not suggested that the needs of a Community Theatre could justify any such elaboration but it is a significant fact that of the 240 dimmer channels available at Stratford no less than 90 are connected to circuits sited in the auditorium: the remaining 150 are distributed above and on the stage. Although our installation would be much more modest the proportions would be about the same.

It is no longer permissible to install the three- or four-compartment battens with three- or four-colour circuits, a compartment footlight, a 12-way spot-bar over the stage, an assortment of floods on stands and, maybe, ten FOH spots on the circle front, an installation that would have been considered fairly lavish in 1932. It is now established practice that the whole of the acting area shall be lit by individual lanterns throwing their beams of light from every possible direction. It is not advisable to be too dogmatic about the number and the specific types of lanterns to be used but one can be fairly definite about the siting and the control of the lanterns. It must be possible for them to be moved easily from one position to another but the need for this interchange, which is time-consuming, should be reduced as far as is possible within the cost limits that may be imposed.

In the case of the Community Theatre, because the use of the lighting will vary considerably, it should be possible to reserve a number of circuits and lanterns for giving adequate general light over the whole of the stage when it is in use for non-theatrical purposes such as concerts, meetings, lectures, etc. These lanterns should be left in more or less permanent positions so that they are always available when needed without somebody having to re-position and to re-focus them, which could be a laborious chore. This may involve some additional capital cost initially but it would be justified by the long-term economy.

Types of Lanterns

Although there is a considerable selection of lanterns with individual characteristics they may be broadly divided into three types. A theatre consultant could provide the necessary expert guidance but the lighting manufacturers could also help when the lighting layout is being prepared.

Profile Spots

These are available in various shapes, sizes and wattages. The profile spot projects a beam with hard edges, the shape of which is determined by the gate aperture, by built-in shutters or by an iris diaphragm which adjusts the diameter of the circle. A variant of this lantern, known as the bi-focal spot, has additional shutters with serrated edges which make it possible for the beam of light to have a combination of hard and soft edges, very useful when pools of light overlap. The profile spot is a very versatile lantern which may be used in various positions. Its main use is in the FOH positions as the comparatively narrow beam is the most suitable for the long throws involved.

Fresnel Spots

This derives its name from the Fresnel lens, which produces a soft-edge spot, the intensity and spread of which is varied by altering the relationship of the lamp to the lens. The larger the diameter of the lens the greater is the light, wattage for wattage.

These spots usually have a wide variation of beam angle and they can be used either to flood a big area or they can concentrate a light of greater intensity on a smaller area. They are sited mainly over the acting area and in the FOH positions nearest to the stage.

Floods

In this category must be included footlights and battens (border-lights) which virtually consist of individual floods welded together. Because any type of flooding equipment has a fixed wide-beam angle it has been largely superseded by the more versatile soft-edge spots for lighting the acting area. In current practice the use of floods is restricted to lighting the cyclorama and any other scenic surface that must be lit at close quarters.

Follow Spots

These high-intensity lights have been most commonly used to follow individual performers about the stage in Variety theatres or, in other theatres, to distinguish the star performers from the hoi polloi of the chorus in musical comedies, or from the corps de ballet. They are an essential part of the performances of pop singers and the like. Formerly the follow spots had carbon arcs as the light sources, as these gave light of a much greater intensity than could be obtained from any lamp then manufactured. The earliest type of electric lamp enclosed a carbon arc, which possibly accounts for uninformed journalists still declaring that certain goings-on were "under the glare of the arc-lights" when it is a safe guess that there were no arcs in the vicinity. Similarly, arcs are still often referred to in the theatre as the "limes," although limelight resulted from a fusion of gas and lime. Arcs had some fire risk and could be quite tricky to use (many are still in use): as the carbons actually burn away they can conk out at inopportune moments if they are not changed in ample time.

It is unlikely that carbon arcs would be supplied to a new theatre as there are a number of different high-intensity lamps available. It is fairly certain that follow spots would be required at times in the Community Theatre and they should be included in the initial list of equipment needed.

Optical-effects Projectors

One hopes that many of the organizations using the theatre for play production will adopt simplified settings and they will probably wish to project effects on the cyclorama or sky-cloth. The projection of clouds, still or moving, transforms the large area of blue light into a convincing theatrical illusion of the infinite space beyond the focal points created by the clouds. The suggestion of a night sky, impossible to create effectively by the popular dark blue that bears no resemblance whatever to any night sky one has seen in this part of the world, can be best indicated by projecting a mass of storm clouds with little, if any, other light on the cyclorama. On a small stage excellent still cloud-projection (and one should mostly use still clouds) can be obtained from a 500-watt profile spot fitted with an extra lens and a mica slide painted with Photopak. For the more ambitious type of optical effects, which are many, there are specially designed lanterns available. The possibility of providing at least one, preferably two, should be considered.

The layout of the lighting equipment, the number and types of lanterns to be provided initially and the circuitry involved need careful consideration at an early stage of the planning. Proper provision must be made to accommodate the equipment during the actual construction of the building.

Siting of Lanterns

There are basic requirements to be borne in mind. It must be possible to light any actor on any part of the acting area and that means the actor's face as well as his feet, which may well be on a rostrum up-stage. He must also be lit from each side so that on any part of the stage there must be light projected from opposing directions. Most of the light will be from overhead positions and, generally speaking, it should be at an angle of 35 degrees to 45 degrees from the horizontal. There will also be need at times for light at shallower angles and possibly at steeper angles. In fixing the overhead positions it must be made possible for the tilt of the lanterns and their lateral movement to be varied without the light being obstructed. Although there are theatre people who do not object to the lanterns being exposed to audience view and, in fact, seem to claim exposure as a functional virtue, if one accepts the need for or the desirability of theatrical illusion one must agree that maximum theatricality is achieved by concealing the light sources; but it is important that concealment must not create obstruction.

FOH Positions

As already stated, a large proportion of the stage-lighting equipment must be positioned in the auditorium. In modern practice these positions are on bridges above ceiling-level and in slots in the side walls. The positions of the bridges and the ceiling apertures must be planned to meet the requirements stated above. Fig. 31 shows in some detail the relationship between the bridge and the aperture to make it possible for the lanterns to be focused and serviced without the acute discomfort that is so frequently caused because it is evidently not realized what physical effort is involved. It must be possible for the operator to work with a full view of the stage without having to be a contortionist. There must be ease of access and room to suspend the largest lantern likely to be used. The operator must have a sense of security when working on the bridge, the floor of which should be timber in preference to metal mesh, which can be murder on the knees. If there is to be an apron stage which can extend the acting area when necessary, some of the lanterns must be so sited that the extension can be properly lit. This will probably involve the provision of a bridge additional to those necessary for lighting the stage without the extension. Although the bridge section shown in Fig. 31 has sloping ceiling panels, they need not necessarily slope. Indeed there are many instances of the suspended ceiling being omitted altogether, leaving the bridge hanging in mid-air. Provided there is suitable

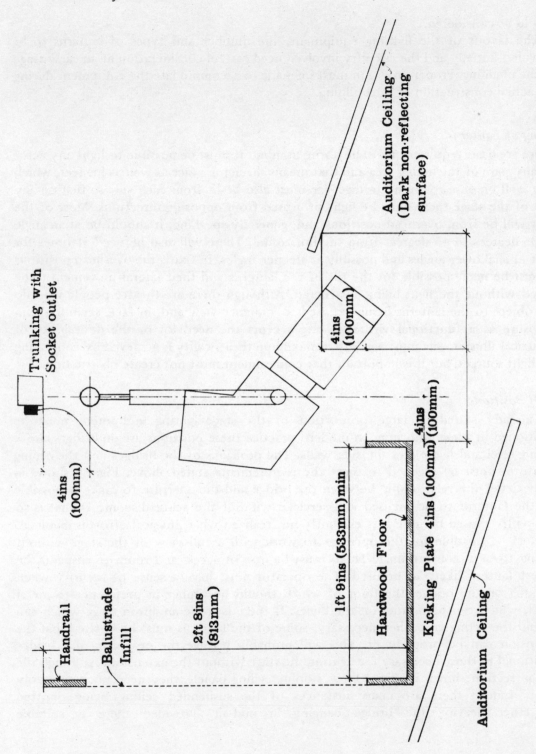

Trunking with
Socket outlet

Handrail

Balustrade
Infill

4ins
(100mm)

2ft 8ins
(813mm)

1ft 9ins (533mm)min

4ins
(100mm)

Auditorium Ceiling
(Dark non-reflecting
surface)

4ins
(100mm)

Hardwood Floor

Kicking Plate 4ins (100mm)

Auditorium Ceiling

*Fig. 31   Section of stage-lighting bridge with minimum measurements recommended by the Association of British
Theatre Technicians.*

down-lighting the lack of a ceiling is not obvious when the auditorium is fully lit. During the performance with the house lights out the positions of the lanterns would be betrayed by the illuminated lenses but when the performance is good enough the attention of the audience would be concentrated on the stage. It is assumed that if the performance is in the round or on a thrust stage care has been taken not to let the light shine in the eyes of the people on the front rows.

In a theatre with proscenium stage the bridges should run the full width of the auditorium to give maximum choice of lighting angles. This would also apply, of course, to the open-end stage. For a thrust stage the siting of the bridges must allow light to be directed to each part of the acting area from three sides instead of two. On a central acting area the actor must be lit from four sides.

The angles of light from the lanterns on the bridges would be in the 35 degrees to 45 degrees range. To meet the need for lower-level lighting at shallower angles wall-slots should also be provided. These vertical positions should, in effect, be a downward continuation of the bridges. Fig. 32 shows the required arrangement of the slots with dimensions. If at all possible there should be rear access to the lanterns in the slots, to avoid the use of ladders in the auditorium which could be quite tricky if used on a ramped or tiered floor on which seating would probably be inconveniently placed. If the rear access is not provided it should be possible to use as steps the horizontal bars to which the lanterns are fixed.

Stage-lighting Control

In current practice it is only for the very small installations that a manually operated switchboard with built-in resistance dimmers could be justifiable. Mass production of thyristor dimmers has made it possible to give remote control of any number of dimmers from six upwards at reasonable prices. These controls are light in weight and small in size, allowing the much easier finger-tip operation. As stated earlier, the operator must be able to see the acting area from either sitting or standing positions. It is worth repeating that the controls and the operator must be as near as possible to the viewing window. Any space for cue sheets, etc., should not intrude between operator and window.

For the type of Community Theatre we have been considering it is probable that there should not be less than 60 dimmer channels with three presets to give smooth transition from one lighting cue to the next one. This is a simple form of control compared with the more sophisticated controls devised for large installations. In British practice it is usual to want a dimmer channel for each lighting circuit. If the number of lighting circuits exceeds the number of dimmer channels provided, possibly to keep down the cost, the former may terminate in a patch panel which permits the selection of any of the circuits up to the total of the dimmer channels available for connection to the control panel. It is rarely if ever necessary to use every lighting circuit at any one

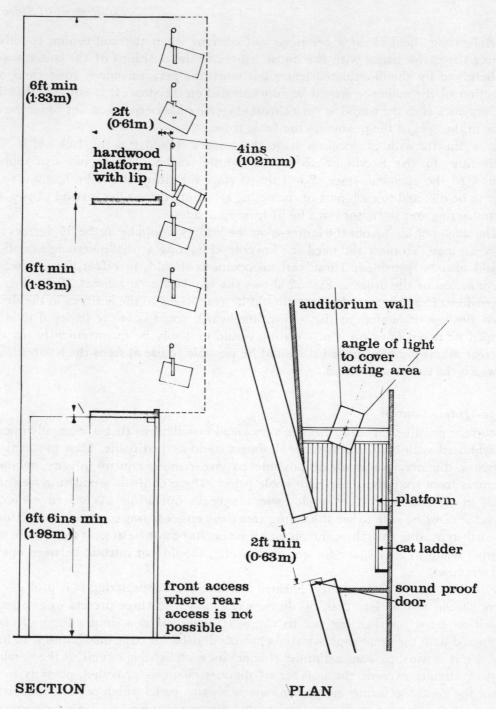

6ft min
(1·83m)

2ft
(0·61m)

4ins
(102mm)

hardwood
platform
with lip

6ft min
(1·83m)

6ft 6ins min
(1·98m)

front access
where rear
access is not
possible

SECTION

auditorium wall

angle of light
to cover
acting area

platform

cat ladder

2ft min
(0·63m)

sound proof
door

PLAN

Fig. 32   Section and plan of auditorium wall slots for stage-lighting equipment, with minimum measurements recommended by the Association of British Theatre Technicians.

time but the circuits needed will vary from one scene to another, which accounts for the growing multiplicity of lanterns and dimmers demanded by lighting designers.

It is not possible or even desirable to offer a standard specification that could be claimed to be suitable for all theatres of a similar type. Opinions of people with comparable experience may differ; their methods of working will also vary quite considerably. Decisions about the number and patterns of lanterns to be supplied, the distribution of the circuits, the number and capacity of dimmers required and the layout of the control are all matters for discussion with those who are familiar with current techniques and practice. A stage consultant should provide architect and client with the independent expertise needed when these decisions have to be made. Light is a vital part of any performance: there are some enthusiasts who say it is the most vital part. It is true that without light the performance would be invisible and theatre cannot usurp the function of radio. "Theatre" means a place for seeing and what is actually seen on the stage is conditioned by subtleties of light and shade and colour devised by the lighting artist: he must be given the right tools to work with.

House Lighting

The auditorium should offer a pleasant welcome to the audience as they enter, preferably at the rear, where they can see rows of seats with the stage beyond. The level of lighting should be adequate for a person with normal vision to read a programme but should not be much higher, if at all. It must be possible for the house lights to fade slowly when the show is about to begin: the eyes must be physically adjusted to the change of intensities if the light on the stage is to register correctly from the start.

Theatre ceilings are no longer ornate and need not be seen: pendant lights are out. Tungsten lamps in simple reflectors should throw the light downwards and as the light sources will not be concealed their brightness should be restrained. In Sheffield's Crucible Theatre, opened in 1972, there are more than 900 individual lamps above the auditorium in an irregular pattern: the visual effect can be quite distressing to the sensitive eye. When down-lighting is used, as in this case, to conceal the lighting bridges, it is theatrical custom to refer to the lights as "blinders": the term should not be taken too literally. "Concealers" might be a more considerate guide to practice.

In a theatre with proscenium and house tabs there should be some equipment reserved for flooding the curtain with light to act as a visual overture. This can induce a valuable emotional stimulus, a stimulus that to some of us with old-fashioned ideas is regrettably lost when there is an open stage, in spite of the use of introductory gimmicks that are often a poor substitute.

(iii) Sound-amplification

Although it should not be necessary to amplify the human voice during most of the activities in the Community Theatre, for some of the activities microphones and loudspeakers—sometimes very loud speakers—are thought to be necessary. Sound equipment has developed a sophistication that is bewildering to the non-expert. The quality of sound has vastly improved if the equipment is controlled sensitively. Careful selection of equipment and its siting must be guided by those who have the technical and operational knowledge.

Siting of the control was discussed earlier (see page 75). Built-in speakers will be needed for the music and other sounds relayed to the audience. Portable speakers with a variety of points at which they may be connected to the system will be needed on stage for "noises off." Twin turntables will be needed for records and as it is now customary for a succession of sound-effects to be transferred to tape in order to simplify operation, there must be tape-recording facilities. It must be possible to store tapes and records near to the control position.

Sound from the stage must be relayed to the control-room: as has been emphasized previously, the operators must work to aural as well as visual cues. It may or may not be thought advisable to relay the stage proceedings to the dressing-rooms but this should not be a substitute for the much more reliable warning of approaching entrances given by the stage manager from the prompt corner. If the performances are relayed to the dressing-rooms he must be able to interrupt the relay with his warnings.

12
Management

The success or failure of any business must depend on the quality of its management. The Community Theatre, which must be run as a business with its own peculiar problems, is no exception.

The overall control may be vested in a Trust formed for the purpose of acquiring and running the theatre, or, if it is owned by a local authority, control may be the responsibility of a Council committee. In either case, although policy will be decided by the controlling body, the detailed working must be delegated to a board of management to whom a general manager is directly responsible. The chairman of the board should be chosen carefully. This chairmanship should not be regarded as an honour to be given for years of devoted service to the community, a kind of long-service medal. It will be an exacting job. The man who takes it on must have a keen interest in the project, some knowledge of the problems likely to arise and the ability to preside with tactful firmness over the deliberations of individuals with contrasting personalities and ideas. He must be able to establish a close and harmonious relationship with the general manager, who will need constant contact on an informal basis in addition to the formal contact at board meetings. The board membership should be kept to a reasonable size, say not less than five or more than seven, and only those people who can undertake to attend meetings regularly should be considered.

The board of management should be appointed immediately a decision has been made to go ahead with the building so that it can function as the client in negotiations with architect, consultants, building and other contractors.

General Manager

One of the most important early jobs of the board should be the appointment of a General Manager. He should be either a man of the theatre with a flair for management or primarily an administrator with a keen interest in and some knowledge of theatre and other forms of entertainment. In either case he (or she) must have a lively personality and the ability to get on good terms with all kinds of people. He must be able to gain the goodwill of the public, the press, the professional and amateur companies likely to use the theatre, and all the local organizations whose co-operation is desirable. He must be able to find suitable attractions and be sufficiently shrewd and tough to negotiate favourable terms with other tough characters. He must be able to organize effective publicity. Contrary to the belief cherished by some performers that it is solely their names and the quality of their performance that brings in the customers, it is the hard work of those who are responsible for selling the show that will produce audiences who have then to be convinced that the show is as good as the performers think it is. If they are convinced they will help to sell the show to others.

If the general manager is as good as he needs to be he will have to be well paid for what is a very full-time job. In the case of a new theatre he should be appointed well in advance of the opening date, by which time the programme for the first few months should have been settled and a lot of public interest generated.

There is a tendency nowadays to adopt such titles as Administrator or Director in preference to General Manager. "Administrator," however, implies a much larger organization than the one we are considering and "Director" could be ambiguous, for that title is now adopted by the person who used to be the Producer. "General Manager" is self-explanatory and the job by any other name would be no more prestigious or less exacting.

Assistant Manager

In a Community Theatre of the type we have in mind the number of staff employed is likely to be limited and the general manager would probably have to undertake detailed work that in a large theatre would be delegated to others. For example, a large theatre might also have a House Manager and a Publicity Manager but it is unlikely that such separate appointments would be justified in our Community Theatre. However, it must be assumed that the general manager will be unreasonable enough to expect to have *some* leisure time to devote to the remnants of his private life and he will need an assistant to whom specific duties could be delegated and who would also have to deputize for the general manager at times. Publicity and house management would probably have to be shared between the general manager and the assistant, each having to take a turn at the very important job of being on view to the public before, during and after each performance, maintaining the friendly relationship between customers and management that is so vital in a theatre of this type.

Clerical Staff

The number of staff required will obviously depend on the nature and extent of the theatre's activities. The general manager will have to decide who does what and how many are required to do it. Somebody will have to do the secretarial and accountancy work and whoever is employed will need to be pretty versatile and not be too concerned about lines of demarcation.

Box-office Staff

The hours during which the box office is open for business will determine the number of attendants required: it is likely that at least two will be needed. Those who do this exacting job should not only be competent but also have a keen interest in whatever is happening in the theatre. The patrons are entitled to expect a sales service that is more personally involved than that given by uninterested assistants handing out pre-packaged goods in a multiple store or supermarket.

Catering Staff

Provision of a restaurant service needs specialized staff and it is not unusual for such a service to be sub-let to a catering firm. If, however, the service is restricted to drinks and snacks the theatre would be well advised to run the bars with its own staff. This may be limited to a full-time manager or manageress and an assistant; additional part-time staff would be employed as necessary. As there will be heavy work involved in restocking the bars and in the removal of the empties each day, it may well be necessary to employ a full-time "handy man."

Cleaners

These would be employed on a part-time basis but it would be necessary to have a full-time Housekeeper with the responsibility for seeing that the whole theatre is kept clean and properly maintained. She may be able to undertake other duties as well.

Usherettes and Cloak-room Attendants

These are likely to be part-time employees. The usherettes would combine programme-selling with directing the customers to their seats but when amateur companies are appearing at the theatre it is more than probable that they would wish to have their own members selling programmes (member participation!).

Stage Staff

Stage Manager

It is necessary to have a full-time manager, preferably one with professional experience and a man who is useful with tools. He would have to co-operate with the stage managers of visiting professional and amateur companies. He must be capable of taking charge of the entire production during performance. His word is law behind the curtain: he must be competent and be seen to be competent by those who have to accept his authority, which includes the performers. He needs discretion, good humour and the calm assurance that prevents him getting into a flap at those critical moments which are occupational hazards.

Electrician
The man appointed should be versatile and fully qualified technically as he will be responsible for all the electrical and mechanical equipment in the theatre. He must be competent to deal effectively with the electronic gadgetry of lighting and sound installations and be able to operate both expertly. He should also have a sensitive appreciation of the subtleties of lighting as he will often have to design stage lighting on his own initiative. He may need a full-time assistant as well as occasional part-timers.

Stage-hands
These are the people who have to do all the stage work other than the electrical jobs, under the direct control of the stage manager. Most of them would be employed on a casual basis, the number varying according to the amount of work involved by the show being presented. It is quite likely that there would have to be a full-time dogsbody and jack-of-all-stage-trades, who would have been known in yesterday's theatre as a "day man" or possibly as "stage carpenter." Included in his many qualifications would be familiarity with the operation and maintenance of any flying system there may be, and he must be able to handle scenery expertly. Amateur companies would usually be willing and anxious to supply volunteer scene-shifters but they would have to work under the supervision of the resident stage staff.

Stage Doorkeeper
It may not be necessary to have a full-time employee for this job but when the theatre is in active use it is important that inquisitive or ill-intentioned persons should be prevented from roaming about the back-stage area. A man who is physically and temperamentally suitable for the job should be recruited.

Preliminary Estimates of Running Costs
It was suggested earlier that the board of management should be appointed as soon as it is decided to proceed with the building. It would be good sense to appoint potential members of the board to an *ad hoc* committee when the project is being considered in general terms. At that stage it is not uncommon for the project to be discussed in very vague terms, with concentration on the obvious practical problems of planning and the raising of funds to meet capital costs, neglecting the equally important problem of how the running costs of the theatre are to be financed when it is built.

The suggested committee should be responsible for preparing estimates of the annual costs likely to be incurred and of the revenue to be expected. The latter will be very difficult to estimate realistically but an attempt should be made. The possible rental charges for the theatre and any ancillary accommodation should be discussed. The rentals would have to be within the financial capacity of the people being catered for. It is useless to be unrealistically optimistic. Some of the amateur companies who may wish to use the theatre could be prevented from doing so if their potential revenue would not balance their overall costs. Uneconomic rentals may be necessary in some cases, or it may be justifiable to fix a modest rental plus a percentage of all receipts over an agreed sum. The terms that would be accepted by touring professional companies will vary according to the status of the company and the type of attraction. They may be willing to operate on a percentage division of gross receipts, with or without a guarantee, or they may be interested only in receiving a fixed sum. In estimating probable attendances it would be rash to expect an average of more than 60 per cent of capacity.

This attempt to estimate the possible revenue of a theatre not actually built can, at best, give only an approximate idea of possibilities, but it is a necessary exercise.

The probable overheads and running costs could be estimated rather more accurately. It should not be too difficult to estimate the approximate costs of salaries, wages, rent (or interest charges), rates, heating, lighting, insurance, printing, publicity, postages, telephones, maintenance and so on. The object is to give those responsible for approving the project a broad indication of the kind of liability that will be incurred when the theatre becomes a reality. One result of the exercise could be to stimulate the planning of additional revenue-producing accommodation to reduce the amount of subsidy necessary. It is most unlikely that the need of a subsidy could be eliminated. Unless there were policy changes and a considerable increase of cash available to the Arts Council, any direct subsidy of running costs from national sources could not be expected. It must be assumed that the local ratepayers will be the reluctant benefactors.

It is now an accepted fact of cultural life in Britain that the arts in general and theatres in particular must be subsidized if they are to survive. The present extent of communal subsidy is not wildly extravagant when measured against the need, but the areas of distribution do not compel universal approval. The theatre is not without its "creative artists" who passionately demand freedom to indulge their creativity, uninhibited by the philistines who insist on counting the cost. It is quite possible that if they were not subsidized and had to work on the old shoe-string they would produce results no worse than when they can cheerfully damn the expense.

When we have to dip our hands into the communal pocket to cater for minority interests, however laudable, there is a moral obligation to try to limit the extractions to a sensible minimum. The subsidizing of theatre or any other cultural or social activity should neither encourage nor excuse reckless extravagance or managerial ineptitude. The extravagance and ineptitude are sometimes complementary but the existence of either or both must not be exaggerated. There is a lot of conscientious competence in the theatre.

Training of Theatre Personnel

By way of a postscript, it may be relevant to the heading of Management to consider the problem of obtaining the qualified people needed in growing numbers to do the specialized and sometimes highly technical jobs in the theatre. There is no lack of drama schools, academies or university departments, but most of the students enrol because they wish to become actors. Quite a number of them fail to make the grade and, by way of justifying the Shavian exaggeration that "he who can does: he who cannot teaches," some of them do try to get jobs in the educational field. Others may wish to become theatre technicians. In the days when theatres were much more numerous it was always possible for those who could find jobs to acquire special skill in the hard school of experience. Because the hours were long and the pay was short, only those who were ensnared by the curious fascination that the theatre has for its slaves were likely to persist. This applied to actors no less than to the less glamorous workers. Now it has become necessary for those who wish to act to have learned something of their craft if they are to be accepted by the theatre and their trade union. Although the training institutions give some technical instruction the main emphasis is usually on acting and production. There is a lack of recognized courses of training for those who wish to start from scratch and to become theatre technicians.

There would seem to be a real need for some kind of national training organization, an institution of theatre technology, comprehensively equipped and staffed to conduct courses of instruction in all the varied techniques except those of acting. In this context it is desirable to interpret "technical instruction" very broadly, for it is not only the potential electrical and stage management personnel who need knowledge of theatre practice. Courses should also be devised to train the artists and craftsmen who wish to design, make and handle scenery and costumes, as well as those who wish to join firms designing, manufacturing and selling theatre equipment. A theatre management course could also be justifiably included in the syllabus.

In addition to the full-time courses, possibly spread over two years, there should be short-term intensive courses devised for special needs. Actors who wish to become directors could be catered for. There should also be holiday courses for amateurs, not with the purpose of attracting them into the professional theatre but to assist them in making their amateur work more efficient and interesting, and special sessions for architectural students and even for qualified architects interested in the design of theatres.

Obviously, such an organization would be costly to create and to maintain: it would have to be nationally sponsored. It would need spacious accommodation. Examples of all kinds of stages would be required and all types of equipment should be available for use in training. It would be essential to provide opportunities for the staging of actual performances to give the trainees practical experience and there should be some association with producing organizations.

Some attempts to deal with the problem have been made. Limited courses have been arranged in a few technical colleges, mainly for trainees, who may already be employed in theatres. Although this may be a useful provision in the London area, where a large number of theatres are within a reasonable radius, the provincial theatres and the potential trainees are very widely scattered about the country, so that the success of such courses will be quite marginal. The problem demands a more ambitious approach on a national basis if there is to be an effective solution.

If there is will enough to find the way there is no reason why such a training organization could not be created, possibly as a separate department of an existing technical college, which would have available qualified electrical and mechanical engineers who could give specialized tuition in techniques adapted to the particular needs of the theatre.

The need for thoroughly trained theatre technicians is just as real as the need for thoroughly trained actors. There are in existence theatre organizations that could do something about this if they were to co-operate with sufficiently energetic enthusiasm. Of course, there is always the risk that such training courses might become standardized and academic and that trainees might become too intent on learning how to teach others who are anxious to learn how to teach others and so on, but that is a risk involved in every type of education. However, there is always a reassuringly large proportion of individualists whose inclinations and ingenuity will make certain that the knowledge gained during training will enable them to develop their own characteristic expertise in doing the actual job.

Because this need exists, something will be done about it—some day!

Greater technical training facilities would not guarantee greater theatre. The amount of educational effort devoted to drama and to theatre in general is greater now than ever before but performance standards of today are not comparatively wonderful. Great theatre is the product of the marriage of technique with genius and some of us who are sliding into the sere and yellow suspect that nowadays there is an excess of technical illegitimacy: we are inclined to assert sadly that things ain't wot they used to be; but, of course, they never were.

Glossary

Act-drop	Now often used instead of House Tabs (q.v.): more correctly used traditionally for the curtain or painted cloth lowered at the end of an act or scene, usually situated behind false proscenium (q.v.) Also known as Front Cloth.
Acting Area	That part of the stage on which the main action takes place, i.e. the part that should be (but often isn't) clearly and completely visible to the whole of the audience.
Actor's Left/ Right	Stage Left or Right from the point of view of the actor facing the audience.
Apron Stage	That part of the stage which extends beyond the House Tabs, however deep or shallow; may be permanent or movable. Often referred to as Forestage, with doubtful authority. OED defines the theatre apron as "The stage area in front of the curtain." (See "Forestage.")
Arena Stage	An acting area completely surrounded by the audience: also known as Theatre in the Round and Centre Stage.
Auditorium	In British usage, the place in which the audience sits: in America, used to describe a theatre which has to serve many purposes, as with our Community Theatre.
Back-cloth	See "Cloth."
Backing	A piece of scenery placed behind any opening in the main setting, i.e. window, door, arch, etc.
Back-stage	The whole of the area outside but adjacent to the stage.
Band-room	Dressing- or rest-room for orchestra. Usually below stage adjacent to orchestra pit.
Barrel	Usually a 2 in. OD gas pipe or alloy tube which is suspended horizontally over the acting area to carry scenery, borders and lighting equipment.
Batten	Length of timber from which scenery, etc., may hang. Lighting batten is a row of lights, usually in compartments, producing a flood of light from above, having three or four circuits to provide choice of colour.
Black-out	Stage lighting out, or possibly a selected group of lights. Dead black-out (DBO) means complete darkness.
Blinders	Originally, lights shining towards the audience to conceal a scene change in a black-out. May mean lights above the auditorium to conceal the bridges and a lack of ceiling.
Book-wing	Two scenery flats hinged together.

Boom	Abbreviation for "boomerang" which, for no obvious reason, means a vertical barrel to which brackets for spot lanterns are fixed. Usually sited in wings (q.v.). A Proscenium Boom is fixed near to proscenium opening. (See "Perch.")
Border	A curtain or painted canvas cloth of restricted height suspended above the stage to mask the tops of the scenery flats and the space above the proscenium opening.
Box Office	The booking office at which the public obtain their tickets: "Box" is much too appropriate much too often.
Box Set	Scenery which creates a room of three walls, the "fourth wall" being the proscenium opening. See page 32 for the alternative room with two walls.
Bridge (Lighting)	A gallery suspended over the auditorium or the stage to give access to lighting equipment. See Fig. 31 page 91.
Centre Stage	See "Arena Stage."
Cloth	(Also known as Drop.) A large painted canvas usually extending beyond the full width and height of proscenium opening. Cut-cloth: one in which there are openings to form arches, etc., or side wings and a border with profiled edges to suggest trees and foliage.
Counterweight System	A method of flying scenery which is counterbalanced by weights loaded in cradles from a loading gallery, and moving vertically in guides on a side wall of the stage. (See "Suspension Gear," page 78.)
Cue	Any audible or visual signal for an appropriate response, e.g. by actor, lighting operator, conductor, etc.
Curtain	Apart from its obvious meaning of suspended draped fabric it is a verbal cue to raise or lower the House Tabs (q.v.) or to draw them on or off.
Cyclorama	(Cyc.) Originally used to describe a semicircular cloth or rigid structure enclosing the acting area. Now applied to a plain framed cloth or a plastered back wall of the stage which can be lit to suggest the sky. If it is a simple back-cloth, possibly painted blue, it would be referred to as a Sky-cloth.
Dimmer	A unit of electrical apparatus inserted in a lighting circuit to permit a lamp or group of lamps to be faded smoothly from nil to full intensity or vice versa, allowing any intermediate intensity to be held in "Check."
Dip	One or a group of socket outlets, usually in the stage floor, having a hinged cover (Trap). Similar sockets situated on the fly-gallery are known as Fly Dips or Fly Plugs.
Director	Now in common use to mean the person previously known in the theatre as Producer, the person who directs the actors and is responsible for the entire production of a show. The change is not without confusing results. Stage Director: the senior stage manager. Artistic Director: the senior producer. Director: may be a general manager or, as in any other business, a member of the Board of a limited company.
Drapes	Any curtains and/or borders which hang in folds.
Drop-cloth	See "Cloth."
End-stage	Usually means a stage which extends the full width between side walls, without a proscenium to divide acting area and auditorium. A platform, in fact.

False Proscenium	An inner proscenium usually situated about 6 ft (1·8 m) up-stage. May be specially constructed or could be created by the Tormentors (q.v.) and a border, behind which are curtains and/or a cloth (Act-drop). Allows scenes to be played on the Forestage (q.v.).
Festoon Curtain	One which is drawn up vertically in folds from bottom to top. Also known as Reefer Curtain. (See Fig. 30 page 83.)
Flat	A piece of scenery, usually rectangular, consisting of a timber frame covered with canvas or possibly hardboard or 3-ply. May have a superimposed profile edge. French flat: a number of single flats battened together to be flown as one piece. (See also "Book-wing.")
Flys	Abbreviation meaning Fly-tower. The space above the stage into which scenery etc. is "flown," i.e. hauled up out of sight. Sometimes wrongly applied to suspended borders and sometimes spelled "flies."
FOH	Abbreviation of Front of House, meaning the whole of the theatre other than the stage area, i.e. auditorium, foyer, bars, etc., particularly the auditorium. Often used to mean the spot lanterns situated in the auditorium.
Footlights	Traditionally "Floats." Rows of lamps, usually in compartments, at the front edge of the stage: rarely installed in new theatres. May be used to light the bottom of a backcloth or cyclorama, when it is known as a Ground-row (q.v.)
Forestage	Often confused with Apron (q.v.). More properly refers to the part of the acting area between the false proscenium (q.v.) and the real proscenium, usually having a depth of about 6 ft (1·8 m). Scenes are often played on the forestage while the main setting is being changed.
Green-room	A retiring- or waiting-room near to the stage. Quite common in the Victorian theatre: now a rarity.
Grid	The framework, formerly of timber but now of steel, to which are fixed the pulleys over which the suspension lines pass when raising or lowering scenery or other equipment. (See "Fly-tower," page 41 and "Suspension Gear," page 78.)
Ground-row	A piece of scenery standing in front of a back-cloth or cyclorama to represent the foreground of the scenic vista. Also used for the compartmented footlight behind the scenic ground-row.
Hemp Lines	Ropes to which scenery is attached for suspension, three in number and known as long, centre and short. Made fast to cleats fixed to a rail on the fly-gallery or on a side wall. Now used mainly on small stages or as supplementary to the counterweighted lines (flexible steel cables) which have largely replaced the ropes.
House Lights	The lights which give general illumination in the auditorium. Also used as a verbal cue for taking out or bringing in those lights.
House Tabs	The curtains which separate the stage from the auditorium, fixed immediately inside the proscenium opening. (See page 82, and also "Act-drop.")
Juliet Balcony	A side balcony in front of the proscenium above an arched opening giving access from stage area to apron. Obviously useful in *Romeo and Juliet* productions.
Lantern (Stage)	See page 77, "Safety-curtain."
Legs	Curtains of restricted width which hang at each side of the acting area, serving as wings (q.v.).

Main Tabs	See "House Tabs."
Off-stage	Means on stage but outside the acting area.
Open Stage	Any type of stage which is within the same structural space as the audience, without separating curtains or proscenium walls.
OP	Opposite Prompt. (See "Prompt Corner" and "Actor's Right.")
Paint Frame	A frame to which cloths or scenery flats are fixed when being painted. Moves up and down in relation to a platform from which the scenic artist works, or, if height is restricted, the platform may move and the paint frame remain stationary.
Pass Door	Door providing access between stage area and front of house.
Pelmet	A border fixed in front of the House Tabs to reduce the effective opening. If placed behind the House Tabs it is known as a Prosc. Border.
Perch	A raised platform behind the Tormentor (q.v.) from which spot lanterns are used to light performers on the forestage. Now largely replaced by Prosc. Booms. (See "Boom.")
Producer	See "Director."
Prompt Corner	The position between the proscenium wall and the setting line (q.v.) occupied by the stage manager or the ASM acting as prompter. Traditionally this is on Actor's Left (Prompt Side). Even if the Prompt Side is on Actor's Right it is quite possible that PS and OP will still be used with the traditional meaning.
Prosc. Boom	See "Boom."
Prosc. Border	See "Pelmet."
Proscenium	Abbreviated: "Prosc." In the modern theatre it means the opening in the wall separating the stage from the auditorium. In Victorian and Edwardian theatres the opening was ornately framed (see Fig. 4(a), page 24), justifying the term "Picture-frame Stage."
Quick-change room	A space on or near to the stage partitioned permanently or temporarily to seclude an actor who has to make a quick change of costume.
Rake	The slope of a floor: often used as alternative to "ramp." The stage floor must not be permanently raked. The auditorium floor should always be raked and, if possible, stepped.
Reefer	See "Festoon."
Revolve	Revolving Stage. A turntable which may be a fixture in the stage floor or may be a temporary structure, allowing a quick change of scene.
Rostrum	A portable platform providing a raised acting level or may be used for stepped seating. For ease of handling and storage may have a loose top and a folding frame. Theatrical plural is "rostrums" but in educational drama there is a fondness for "rostra."
Safety-curtain	See page 77.
Setting Line	The point up-stage at which the scenery begins. If tormentors (q.v.) are used they would fix the setting line: otherwise a "return" flat would serve the same purpose.
Sight-line	An uninterrupted line of sight to the acting area from the eyes of a person seated in the auditorium. See page 20.

Slot	Aperture in side wall of auditorium in which spot lanterns may be fixed vertically, providing low-level stage lighting to supplement lighting from above, ususally desirable if footlights are not used.
Spot	A focus lantern, with many varieties. (See page 87.)
Stage-cloth	See page 85.
Stage Manager	The man who is in complete charge of the stage during performances and in control of all personnel concerned with the production.
Tabs	See "House Tabs." Often used instead of "curtains," particularly if they are Trailers (q.v.). Also the name of the lively quarterly journal published by Rank Strand Electric.
Theatre in the Round	See "Arena Stage."
Thrust Stage	See page 11.
Tiers	Applied to the different levels of seating, e.g. Circle, Balcony, Gallery. May also mean a stepped auditorium.
Tormentor	Two flats fastened together at right-angles, sited at each side of the proscenium opening. One flat having an arched entrance to the forestage. See "False Proscenium" and "Forestage."
Trailers	A pair of curtains which are pulled on and off stage on a suspended curtain-track: may be operated by endless hand-rope or by winch and steel cable.
Transverse Stage	A centre stage with two opposing banks of seats. Alternative to Theatre in the Round.
Trap	See page 73. Also see "Dip."
Trip	To raise a cloth by top and bottom battens on two sets of lines so that the flying space occupied is only half of the height of the cloth.
Tumble	To roll up a cloth on a large diameter roller operated by a rope line, as an alternative to flying or tripping when height above stage is restricted.
Wings	The space between the acting area and the side walls. Also means single flats or leg curtains placed at an angle at each side of the acting area to create entrances. Wood-wings: painted trees; profiled. Book wings: two flats hinged together.

Book List

(A few of the many books dealing with theatre subjects, selected as having some relevance to the Community Theatre.)

The Theatre Today in England and Wales.   (Arts Council of Great Britain)
The report of an Arts Council Theatre Inquiry in 1970.

New Theatres in Britain.   (Rank Strand Electric Ltd.)
A selection of plans and photographs of 78 new theatres built between 1957 and 1970, most of which had been previously reviewed fully in TABS, the quarterly journal edited by Frederick Bentham who has written a lengthy and characteristic introduction.

Theatre Planning.   Edited by Roderick Ham (Architectural Press)
This is the most comprehensive and informative examination of the problems involved in the planning of theatres ever published in this country. A more modest version was originally published in 1964 in co-operation with the Association of British Theatre Technicians. To anybody who may be concerned with the planning of a Community Theatre this new book is indispensable.

New Theatre Forms.   Stephen Joseph (Pitman)
A compressed survey of the development of the proscenium theatre and a detailed examination of the various types of open stages that should be considered as alternatives.

Actor and Architect.   Edited by Stephen Joseph (Manchester University Press)
Report of a symposium organized by the Manchester University Drama Department in 1962.

Proscenium and Sight-lines.   Richard Southern (Faber & Faber)
A thoroughly practical book which examines in very precise detail the problems of masking on the proscenium stage.

Small Auditoriums with Open Stages.   James Hull Miller (Hub Electric Inc. USA)

Self-Supporting Scenery.   James Hull Miller (Published by the author in Shreveport, La., USA)
These are complementary publications. Miller has designed many open stages all over the USA, presupposing the use of free-standing scenery in a sculptural manner as distinct from the perimeter settings used on the proscenium stage. Practical, informative and original.

The Art of Stage Lighting.   Federick Bentham (Pitman)
Published in 1971, it is an updated replacement of the Bentham book of 1954 and has become the acknowledged authority on the design and use of stage lighting equipment. The new book has the added authority of maturity and is as informative to technicians as to theatre artists.

Scene Painting and Design.   Stephen Joseph (Pitman)
As may be expected by those who knew the author, this is a stimulating and versatile treatment of the subject by a man who, in a life all too short, did almost every job in the theatre: manager, stage director, producer, scenic artist, lighting designer, university lecturer and the British apostle of theatre in the round. His comments on scene design are not restricted to the proscenium stage.

Theatre Administration.   Elizabeth Sweeting (Pitman)
A practical guide to theatre management in general and in detail, based on wide experience and written with authority. Essentially a book of reference for anybody who is or hopes to be connected with the management of any type of theatre.

British Theatre Directory.   (Vance-Offord Publications Ltd., Eastbourne)
A comprehensive directory of Theatres, Concert Halls, Producing Companies, Agents, Publishers, Consultants, and the various Councils, Associations, Societies and other organizations concerned with various theatre matters.

Theatre Directory: Suppliers and Organizations   (Stacey)
Specially devised for amateur theatre groups. Classified sections include: Publishers and Agents; Costumes and Scenery; Furniture and Props; Stage Lighting; Sound Effects; Insurance; Magazines; Drama and Music Festivals; Theatre Guilds; Drama Advisers; Training Schools and Courses; etc. Published every two years. The 1972/73 edition at 20p. is extremely good value.

Index